BwB 2019
Keep.

OKANAGAN COLLEGE LIBRARY

03812575

D0609615

Seeing Stars

OKANAGAN COLLEGE
LIBRARY
BRITISH COLUMBIA

Seeing Stars

Spectacle, Society and Celebrity Culture

Pramod K. Nayar

$SAGE Los Angeles • London • New Delhi • Singapore • Washington DC
www.sagepublications.com

Copyright © Pramod K. Nayar, 2009

All rights reserved. No part of this book may be reproduced or utilised in any form or by any means, electronic or mechanical, including photocopying, recording or by any information storage or retrieval system, without permission in writing from the publisher.

First published in 2009 by

 SAGE Publications India Pvt Ltd
B1/I-1 Mohan Cooperative Industrial Area
Mathura Road, New Delhi 110 044, India
www.sagepub.in

SAGE Publications Inc
2455 Teller Road
Thousand Oaks, California 91320, USA

SAGE Publications Ltd
1 Oliver's Yard, 55 City Road
London EC1Y 1SP, United Kingdom

SAGE Publications Asia-Pacific Pte Ltd
33 Pekin Street
#02-01 Far East Square
Singapore 048763

Published by Vivek Mehra for SAGE Publications India Pvt Ltd, typeset in 10.5/13pt Georgia by Excellent Laser Typesetters, Delhi and printed at Chaman Enterprises, New Delhi.

Library of Congress Cataloging-in-Publication Data

Nayar, Pramod K.
    Seeing stars: spectacle, society and celebrity culture/Pramod K. Nayar.
        p. cm.
Includes bibliographical references and index.
    1. Popular culture.   2. Celebrities.   3. Celebrities in mass media.
4. Mass media and culture.   I. Title.

HM621.N39   306.0954—dc22   2009   2008048926

ISBN: 978-81-7829-907-5 (PB)

The SAGE Team: Elina Majumdar, Maneet Singh, Gautam Dubey
                    and Trinankur Banerjee

Contents

Preface

This schematic book provides a set of approaches and frames for interpreting Page 3 people (P3P).

It suffers from the usual flaws of an introduction—it is a collage of analyses of diverse things or basically things that interest *me*. In any case, since celebrity culture is inherently rhizomatic and draws upon multiple sites and forces, from media representations to public events to material products cast in their name, there cannot be any one route into the phenomenon. This is the precise point to set the reader thinking about scandals and famous bodies, fashion and spectacles involving hyper-visible and ultra-recognisable faces. To this end the sources come from gossip magazines, tabloids, television, talk shows, newspapers and films. (I dearly wanted to do comic book celebrities but I could not persuade anyone that purchasing vast numbers of comics was an academic project.) Shah Rukh Khan and J Lo, *Bigg Boss* and Beckham, Tendulkar and *Indian Idol* all find space here.

The celebrity, you might say, is writ large. A celebrity is a spectacle. This book locates stars as spectacles that consumers view, adore and fantasise about. It treats the celebrity as a congeries, a construct of many elements—what it calls celebrity ecology—and examines some of these in detail. The culture of celebrity is, as the book demonstrates, never unified or unproblematically direct. It is multi-faceted, schismatic, polymorphous and, despite all this or perhaps because of popular. In its approach to celebrity culture, *Seeing Stars* is located firmly within the realm of Cultural Studies and explores different features of a very common phenomenon in public culture. The book is also as a congeries of sorts, often moving rapidly, mostly weaving through many features and signs of the texts of celebrity culture.

There are plenty of stars here and, as the chapter titles suggest, the book explores various dimensions of these glamorous, bright, often exploding, distant stars that are part of our everyday lives. *Seeing Stars* attends solemnly to the media rituals, from contests to talk shows and Reality TV shows, and consumer culture that enables the construction of celebrities (Chapter 2: 'A Star is Born: Constructing Celebrity'). It stares in awe and cheers at the performances that make celebrities spectacles for the masses and can, on occasion, even make the ordinary into a celebrity (Chapter 3: 'Star Power: The Celebrity as Spectacle'). It lingers, with vicarious pleasure, at the sites of scandals haunting celebrities that mar the visages of stars (Chapter 4: 'Star Spotting: Celebrity and Scandal'). Finally, *Seeing Stars* turns the spotlight away from the stars to see what the audience is doing as it stares, devours and creates its own scripts about the stars—the audience and fan consumption of celebrities (Chapter 5: 'With Stars in Our Eyes: Consuming Celebrity').

While the examples, which in a rapidly changing context such as celebrity culture are necessarily topical but ephemeral, are drawn mainly from Indian contexts, the book is not restricted to them. There is a definite reason for this. In the globalised world of heavily mediated lives in metropolises, celebrities cut across cultural and geographical formations. There is now a vertical, horizontal and multi-directional integration of cultural icons, artifacts and themes. JLo and Tiger Woods have arguably the same degree of visibility as Shah Rukh Khan (SRK) (recall the crowds at Warwick Castle [UK] to greet SRK, June 2007), and Sachin Tendulkar; note the crowds around Brad Pitt and Angelina Jolie during their 2007 India visit. Indian celebrities wear exclusive foreign brands and are reported in magazines, and metropolitan college students know Eminem's latest song. Celebrity culture, produced, disseminated and consumed through global media is a truly global culture now.

However, the ephemeral nature of adverts means that by the time this book is in print, some of the examples might be retrievable only through the archives.

Okay, we are done with the talking, now let's get this show on the road.

PKN
Hyderabad
2007–2008

Acknowledgements

'A slim, smart, retail book on celebrity culture', said Ashok Chandran at SAGE. 'An introduction', I said, worried as to what he meant by a *retail* book. 'Sure, and in a graphic format?' he queried. 'Not a coffee-table work', I said, now worrying about both retail and graphic (as an academic given to quibbling over semantics, I was horrified by the suggestion that the second term evoked). 'No, no, not at all, but lay off the jargon, please', he said, happy to have found a quiescent academic, but no doubt secretly worrying about my ability to turn off the tap of academic jargon. This book took shape across several such emails and discussions, which sometimes threatened to create at least three different books. My deep gratitude to Ashok for his hyper-enthusiastic receptivity to the idea of this book, his encouragement, constructive comments, and refreshingly quirky take on things. And no, Ashok, I have not used the word 'interpellated' even once (except here, I think).

Then Ashok decided that he had had enough of my writing and set out to do some of his own. Here Elina Majumdar steps in. Skillfully, cheerily, efficiently, Elina guided this book through to its final version. This book's final form owes much to her guiding hand (and the delete key). And the minute it was done, the day I sent off the revised manuscript for refereeing, Elina (who, like me, seems to have an aversion to my getting time off from work) promptly queried me about the *next* book I could do.

I am linguistically challenged when it is time to express my gratitude to my colleague and friend, Anna Kurian. Anna, now of a despondent disposition from having read my weak sentences for five—no, six—years now, read the manuscript, offered suggestions, engaged in debates, phoned/texted whenever she found suitable TV shows and, despite being an Indian academic affiliated with an English department, trawled (only) refereed journals for useful essays. To her I owe much of my thinking. I do hope this book is worthy of you, A.

Narayana Chandran is arguably the academic with the greatest quantum of news about fellow academics, but is also (for me) a free bibliographic search service hosted by the University of Hyderabad. He embeds his astute observations in thrilling gossip, conducted over the noise in rackety buses, which de-celebratises celebrity academics and colleagues. For this I am very grateful because he sets me thinking, even though he might get me to hold mutually contradictory ideas in my head simultaneously. If you are embarrassed by what I have done, Professor KNC, the inadequacies are the effect of what I did with the search service.

I am grateful to the reviewer of the manuscript for a very close reading, constructive suggestions and encouraging remarks.

Professor Richard Fox sent me his exciting paper, 'Jesus as Celebrity', and set me thinking along various lines: my thanks to him for this generous gesture.

My five and a half year-old son, Pranav, posed a key question: 'Why don't you retire NOW—then you won't have to go to the university, teach, attend meetings and get tired, and then you can write *more* books, nah?' (conversation of 5.43 P.M.–5.55 P.M., 5 September 2007, Teacher's Day). Yet he politely declined my request to compose a letter to my Vice Chancellor requesting an extended leave of absence for me to write. Sigh. Bustling around with assorted *fixoes* and Power Rangers, and explaining elaborate stories of their surpassingly tedious lives battling weird, demonic forces to his slow parent—it took me some time to recognise 'Ben 10'—he finally gritted his teeth, rather as I do with my students when explaining the (absence of?) finer points in William Wordsworth, and provided the necessary distraction. Thank you, young P.

My parents, now with perpetual anxiety writ on their faces at my excessive work and minimal sociability, offer prayers and support, unstinted and undiluted. To them, my gratitude, as always.

Ajeeth, himself busier than ever, claims I am more unavailable than he is (an outrageous untruth), but ensures that the friendship endures with his phone calls (that open with 'kahaan hai re bhai tu?'). I am very grateful for this.

Niyati, despite her health and because of her loyalty, perused chapters and offered comments (mixing it up with bits from whatever she was reading at the time). Thank you, once again.

Neeraj and Claire Khadakkar—thank you for converting your home in Boulder, Colorado, into my offshore *drop box* for books purchased.

The American Information and Research Centre (Chennai) and its ever-reliable Mr Jagadish Mysore, supplied books and articles with their quiet efficiency. It is a privilege to acknowledge them.

Colin Harrison, at Liverpool John Moores University, is a regular and uncomplaining supplier of materials and to his encouragement and *supplies*, I owe so much. Thank you, Colin (and this is a gentle reminder: please don't flag in these acts of generosity!).

Sri Anil and Smt Nilima Khadakkar, my parents-in-law, uncomplainingly increased their baggage weight, and whose suitcases bulged in unsightly ways as a result while returning from the US of A, carting a dozen heavy books for me. Thank you!

Finally, Nandini, often felt as a whirring in the vicinity as she flies around the house negotiating her own work schedule more diverse than mine. Ever encouraging, eager to show me one more ad or TV item for analysis, for her quiet affection and what is now her widely celebrated efficiency: much much gratitude.

Parts of this book were delivered as lectures at the Mudra Institute of Communications, Ahmedabad (MICA), June 2008. I am grateful to Atul Tandan, Director, MICA, and Rita Kothari for their gracious invitation and warm hospitality. Thanks also to students of the PGCM-X course, especially Pranay Singh, Bharati Athlekar, Rahul Fernandes, Varun Shourie, Sunder Raj Iyer, Rashmi Krishnamurthy and Anbazhagan Elango, for their enthusiastic interaction, comments and often puzzled queries at the 'semiotics of celebrity culture'. I would also like to thank Anupam, Payal, Trinankur, Rachna, Gautam and the entire SAGE team for their work on this book.

1

Who Wants to be a Celebrity?

We live in a culture of celebrity. From P3Ps to endorsements, from movie stars to television personalities, from comic book celebrities to notorious scamsters. Celebrities, one might say, are everywhere.[1] They haunt the news reports, occupy prime time television, sizzle on multiplex screens and stare at you inside autorickshaws and hair cutting salons. They sell products, events and services. Even when they deny, or especially when they do, that they are celebrities and disparage P3 culture, as the poet Imtiaz Dharker and her daughter, actress Ayesha Dharker, did recently in *The Hindu*, they attract attention as celebrities![2] Some spread AIDS awareness or work for the homeless; other celebrity scamsters make millions by bending the law or exploiting the poor; they battle pollution or they may shoot endangered animals; they lead austere lives, reflecting the social conditions of millions of Indians or they may be given to ostentatious displays of their wealth. Celebrities may play many roles and serve many purposes. They become the voice of the marginalised, a new 'behalfism', as Salman Rushdie calls it (Rushdie 2002: 60), and the exploited, taking up assorted public causes like Arundhati Roy, Medha Patkar, Shabana Azmi and Swami Agnivesh. Or they tie up with the industry and capitalism and become the sales personnel for various products like Shah Rukh Khan (SRK) and Sunfeast biscuits, Sania Mirza and Sprite, Saif Ali Khan and Colgate. Medha Patkar and development, Arundhati Roy and anti-nuclearism, Abdul Kalam and schooling, Lalu Yadav and Harvard...the list is unending and diverse and includes global faces like Paris Hilton, David Beckham, Brett Lee, Arnold Schwarzenegger, Shakira and Bill Clinton. It would be no exaggeration to say that today you cannot *avoid* seeing a celebrity.

This book treats celebrity culture *as a part of everyday life and culture*, the constituent of our visual fields in the form of hoardings or endorsements or TV (this is my first assumption). Celebrity culture is inextricably linked to everyday life through a feedback loop in a recurrent linkage. Celebrities

1. circulate as images in everyday life and public space,
2. thrive on the response these images invoke and circulate even more as a result.

This assumption suggests that we need to see celebrity culture as constituted not only by the celebrity bodies and the media productions of the bodies but also through the consumption by audiences that in turn fuels further media production and circulation. Celebrity culture cannot, clearly, be studied without accounting for the reception of celebrities. The mechanics of celebrity culture involve both production and consumption as integral to the process of 'celebrity-dom'.

My second assumption is that *celebrity culture is a process where the completely bizarre is rendered familiar and yet remains distant* in terms of the possibilities of our acquiring the same status, wealth, looks or power. The lifestyle of the rich and famous, whose lives are led in contexts very far removed from the adoring millions, are rendered familiar to us through the media. Celebrity culture is rooted in the everyday through this process where the celebrities are placed as simultaneously *distant and familiar*. This is an effect of particular processes that involve media productions and reception by audiences.

A third assumption is that *celebrity culture is the effect of mass media*. That is, celebrity culture cannot be separated from various technologies of representation, like the media, cinema, TV, websites, where the media seeks to disseminate the representation to the largest possible audience. Although celebrities existed before the age of TV and the Internet, the circulation of magazines and tabloids in print culture ensured that monarchs, statesmen and great artists remained in the public eye. What we see today is an extension of print culture's celebrity obsession from earlier times. The new forms of celebrity culture, such as talk shows, websites and endorsements, are extensions of similar, earlier efforts at building a public image. Monarchs sought popularity by ensuring that their exploits were sung and exhibited in all corners of their empire. Print enabled visual and literary descriptions. Stage shows and public spectacles showcased their family and achievements.

What is it about celebrity culture that copious amounts of time, energy, planning and money are spent on a few select faces that are then reproduced endlessly in many types of media? What makes some faces and bodies celebrities? What contexts produce celebrities? And who watches them? What kind of power does a celebrity possess? Are they simply representations of collective desires and anxieties of looking good, being talented, being attractive or are they the result of careful marketing strategies that have sold specific looks and talents as being valuable? What is the *ecology* of the celebrity?

This book explores the production, circulation and consumption of celebrities through varied examples and frames. It sees celebrity culture as a phenomenon that exists in every domain, even as celebrities themselves cross domain borders. The book therefore looks at different kinds of celebrities in order to see the operations of celebrity culture; for example, authors like Vikram Seth, Ramachandra Guha, Arundhati Roy, Salman Rushdie; activists such as Medha Patkar; film stars namely, SRK, Amitabh Bachchan, Aishwarya Rai; sports stars like M.S. Dhoni, Sachin Tendulkar; television personalities, Smriti Irani, Aman Verma; and the victimised like Mohammed Haneef, the terror suspect who was arrested by Australian authorities and was the centre of global protest.

The most unique feature of celebrity culture today, especially in metropolises after the advent and spread of mass media, is its global nature. Youth in metropolises are as familiar with Western stars, like footballer Beckham, Formula 1 racer Michael Schumacher, pop star Britney Spears and heiress Paris Hilton as they are with Indian celebrities like SRK, Tendulkar and Arundhati Roy. Global media in fact is united not only in its imperialist survey of poverty, war zones and militarisation but also through fashion, lifestyles and celebrity culture. Celebrity culture cuts across linguistic, regional and national borders and global figures or icons share the pedestal with more local celebrities. This is the *verticality* of celebrity culture where the circulation-reception of celebrities often moves through the scales of development and economy, as in the First World and Third World, upper class and lower class, and integrates diverse, often uneven, cultures into the fold of celebrity culture.

Defining Celebrity

Who or what is a celebrity? A quick answer would be that a celebrity is an individual or event that the public watches: someone or something that is recognised by a large number of people. On an individual level, celebrity culture is the consequence of a *public* recognition of some qualities that a person possesses or is deemed to possess. Celebrity is thus closely aligned with *public* culture and *public* awareness of the work of the individual, which also means that celebrity culture is rooted in everyday, mass culture where the reception of icons enables further and greater circulation. Celebrity culture is about *meanings*, where some individuals command the attention of large numbers of people, who seem to find special qualities or meanings in them. Celebrities give the public pleasure, pain or suffering with their actions, and win adulation or opprobrium accordingly. When Tendulkar does not score, or when he gets out in the 1990s in one-day internationals, as was the case through most of 2007, the country as a whole grieves. When Lalu Yadav turns the fortune, both economic and status-wise, of the largest public sector undertaking, the Indian Railways, it amazes all of India. When Mukesh Ambani and Lakshmi Mittal make it to the Forbes list of millionaires, many newspapers express a sense of pride. Celebrities clearly serve an important social purpose—their actions generate emotional effects on a large number of people.

It is instructive to note the terms used to describe the Mittals, Mallyas and Birlas as corporate moguls, liquor barons and steel 'kings'. The terms indicate a lineage for the celebrity—they are the *new* emperors within capitalism that create the new monarchy of entrepreneurs and industrialists. The ecology of the industrial celebrity, with its links to the bio-, industrial, financial and political system, is this new monarchy. The ecology of the film or sporting celebrity is also this new monarchy of achievement, looks, abilities and power.

We all recognise Anil Ambani, Lakshmi Mittal, Ratan Tata, Vijay Mallya and Yash Birla. Despite this enviable visibility, as a prominent magazine put it, reveals 'some secrets about their personalities that are hitherto unknown … intimate, personal and extremely guarded'. These secrets are their spiritual interests, which magazines reveal for the public.[3] But why would we be interested in whether Anil Ambani does two-hour *puja* everyday or Salman Khan is a devout Muslim? Critics have argued, correctly, that an individual becomes a celebrity only when the public begins to take a keen interest in her or his personal life (Rojek 2001). A celebrity is one whose private life acquires as much public importance, and into which people want sights and insights, as her or his public one. Thus we all want to know about Tendulkar's family, SRK's courtship of Gauri in the 1980s,[4] Sania's taste in clothes or the scandals in Aishwarya Rai's life. Sensationalist articles with leading titles like 'The Pakistani Doctor Diana Loved and Lost' entice us with the secret lives of particular individuals, marking them out as celebrities.[5]

We can also refer to SRK or Tendulkar or M.S. Pandher or Smriti Irani as famous, stars (though the term is almost always linked to the film field) or well known. Each one of these is well known for a particular expertise, work or achievement often of the dubious kind, for instance, the paedophilic murder-crimes of M.S. Pandher and Surinder Kohli, and more recently, in the European context, Kate McCann and the death of their child in 2007. In Daniel Boorstin's definition dating back to the 1960s, 'the celebrity is a person who is known for his well-knownness' (Boorstin 1961: 57).

Well-known is often a tag that is synonymous with fame. Increasingly, fame, renown and celebrity are used interchangeably, though there is a fine distinction between them. Fame was, in earlier eras, the consequence of deeds and achievements (the hero), while celebrity is the consequence of publicity and well knownness. This shift from fame to celebrity is crucial because the latter gestures at the media-driven recognisability of some people (Braudy 1986: 562; Schmid 2006: 298). Thus Nathuram Godse who killed Mahatma Gandhi arguably has the same degree of *media visibility* and *recognisability*, albeit a notorious one, as his famous saintly victim, even though his reputation is predicated upon and derived from his more illustrious victim. Likewise the assassins of Abraham Lincoln (John Wilkes Booth) and John F. Kennedy (Lee Harvey Oswald) retain, decades later, a high degree of visibility in public memory for their reprehensible acts of violence. Though it must be said that the victim's celebrity status survives *longer* than the assassin's, thus suggesting a hierarchy of celebrity-dom, and the killer of a famous icon feeds off the celebrity-hood of the victim. With the mass media of the post-1980s the serial killer, the master crook and the sports star are all equally well-known. If fame, which originally meant 'of good reputation' continues to have a sense of achievement and glory attached to it, celebrity now increasingly means recognisability, visibility and mass media coverage.

An individual therefore becomes a celebrity only when she or he is acknowledged in the public realm as possessing something special. But how do we *know* that X or Y possesses something unique, something above the ordinary? How does a villager in rural Andhra Pradesh know that Sachin Tendulkar is a fine batsman or that SRK, described as 'the world's biggest film star' by UK's respected newspaper *The Guardian* is a star?[6] Does the knowledge about every celebrity circulate in the same way? Is Medha Patkar as well known a celebrity as Tendulkar or SRK?

This book tries to explore and answer these and other questions in the next few chapters. What it does *not* do—and I shall reserve that for another book—is to distinguish *between* celebrities and their specific features, such as the sports stars and masculinities, the rock stars and substance abuse, the politicians and nationalism. It is possible, this book demonstrates, how to read celebrity culture as a whole, while keeping in mind that there are internal variations in each form.

Celebrities are people recognised widely. They are commodities and effects that are produced by mass media image-making (representations), are consumed by large audiences who take an interest in their personal as well as public life, and who project, promote or present themselves in particular or spectacular ways for this consumption to take place. Celebrities serve a social function because of their cultural, symbolic, economic and political power, which is constantly enforced and reinforced through mass media representations. They are both, real people with particular talents and the effect of media generated information or hype *about* these talents where the information makes the audience believe that these talents are to be valued. Celebrities establish norms for looks, behaviour, wealth and success, and become models for emulation.

From this extended definition, two points about celebrity culture emerge. First, celebrities are created by a public awareness of the actions of certain individuals and, second, this public awareness is made possible by the mass media.

Celebrity culture is possible *only* in the age of mass media. Celebrities require the mass media to circulate their images and talk about them. Celebrities are constructed through this process of talking, exchange of information and public visibility. Let us take an example that illustrates this point. In ancient India,

Emperor Ashoka had acquired considerable renown. But how many of his subjects knew what he *looked* like? They had heard of him, they served him and were affected by his decisions. But was there a face they could ascribe to this great King?[7] The issue of the looks of a renowned king is more complicated than it appears. In fact this look-alikeness was complicated enough for Santosh Sivan and Shah Rukh Khan (SRK) when they were planning *Asoka* (2001). When asked if he would do the title role and play the great king, SRK is reported to have asked Santosh Sivan, 'Why me? Do I look like him?' Anupama Chopra, who reports this conversation, notes that there are 'few historical records that authentically establish what Ashoka looked like'! (Chopra 2007: 191)

In contrast, we have Abdul Kalam or Manmohan Singh or George Bush, Jr. Arguably, these people occupy positions of power comparable to former kings and queens. The difference is that a vast majority of people can recognise the face of the President or Prime Minister of the country, thanks to news items on nationwide television programmes, movie clips, websites (a relatively urban phenomenon thus far) and visual material of assorted types. Celebrity status relies heavily on this recognisability and in this the mass media proves indispensable. Mass media reaches out to more people than ever before and transmits both elite and popular culture.

It could be argued that print achieved this reach even before the advent of the Internet. In fact, print, as Elizabeth Eisenstein has shown (1979), did *popularise* a variety of images, texts and beliefs in early modern Europe, from the Bible to the ballads about heroes and events, and products to imperial achievements. Print transformed the popular culture of early modern England and bestowed visibility upon people and events. The mass media of today extends in unprecedented ways this phenomenon of technology-driven celebrity-dom. Furthermore, it could also be argued that there has always been an audience for celebrities, even before the advent of electronic media. Celebrities circulated through minstrelsy, bardic songs, imperial arches (especially in England, as Richmond Barbour,

2003, has demonstrated) and reports of royal festivities. Celebrities might have had a local following as opposed to a global recognition and visibility then. There is thus a history of celebrity consumption that climaxes in the new media blitz common today, but this history is not one that this book explores. (It has been extensively studied in Leo Braudy's pioneering work of 1986.)

In an elite metropolitan environment, especially with the advent of widely publicised advances, Booker Prize lists advertised in Crossword and other book stores, readings in elite hotels, high profile book launches, newspaper writings and interviews, the literary author is also now a celebrity, both locally and in the global literary marketplace (for example, writers such as Salman Rushdie, Arundhati Roy, Kiran Desai, Vikram Seth, Ramachandra Guha). Celebrity authors, as Joe Moran argues, occupy an interesting location in society. They are crossover successes, emphasising both marketability and traditional cultural hierarchies in the blurred zone between 'the legitimacy of culture and the less ambiguous sanction of the marketplace' (Moran 2000: 6). Roy in particular, with just one Booker-winning novel to her credit, has commercial value and is an extremely media-savvy activist. Rushdie is the controversial author who may be credited with having put Indian writing in English on the global map. Ramachandra Guha, one of India's finest historians, likewise, has attained a significant celebrity status through his justly famous works, journalism and well-publicised book releases. As I write in 2007, Guha's *India After Gandhi* occupies best-seller lists in India. The author is thus respected for her or his work and recognised through extensive media coverage that generates both marketability for the author and a star system in the cultural arena. Star authors are not only recognised for their contribution to culture and tradition, and thereby claimed as *national* icons, but also as highly marketable commodities. They possess both economic and cultural capital. The author is involved (Salman Rushdie and Arundhati Roy are excellent examples here) in both promotion and self-promotion, where the public image or construction of the author is closely monitored and even contributed to by the author herself or himself through self-promotion (what Moran terms as 'symbiotic relationship') (Moran 2000: 23).

So, a celebrity is at least partly the effect of the media's continuous representation of her or his qualities and there is no celebrity culture without media culture.

This does not mean that celebrities are only the result of media manipulation of sensibilities or that they are worthless in their own right. What I want to emphasise is that a celebrity is one *only so long as the media generates an enormous amount of information*—visuals, gossip, news—about her or his worth so that the public domain is full of that individual. In effect, therefore, celebrities are supported by their audiences who *consume* their icons and ironically keep them alive through this consumption.

The third point that emerges is that if the celebrity is an effect of media representation, then the *nature* of this representation is crucial to celebrity culture. Mass media tells us so and so is a good player, an important leader or a brilliant criminal. The media clearly positions the individual in a certain light for her or him to be consumed and recognised as a celebrity.

The media *sells* us a personality to consume, but it sells us what we *want* to consume. It channelises our abstract desire and focuses on the celebrity's wealth, looks and power as worth *envying*, *striving for* and *fantasising about*. They give a shape to the audience's amorphous desires, making her or him say, '*this* is what/who I want to be'. Celebrity culture therefore hinges upon both the voyeuristic *consumption* of a media image (celebrity reception) and the goal-setting *production* of the same (celebrity spectacle).

If so, in what way is this media representation different from promotional material like advertisements, which also tell us that a particular product is good for us? There is little difference between promoting a celebrity and promoting a product because both use similar forms of praise, efficiency or importance in their representation of their chosen objects. The celebrity is also a commodity that is *represented* and *promoted* as important or attractive by the media. In other words, celebrities are *products* of promotional campaigns and the subject of promotional material like any other commodity. They are *materials* to be branded and sold. Fame is a manufactured product, manufactured in and by the mass media for public consumption.

Almost every English-language newspaper in India today carries a party page where the local celebrities, or those whom we should assume are celebrities, figure. *Society* magazine runs a 'Party Central' column where the rich and famous are showcased, with some personal information (somebody has shed some weight) and some surpassingly banal comments ('X and Y appeared oblivious to the world'). *Hi! Blitz* had its 'Hi! Couple' series in the May 2007 issue, assuming that we would all want to know the best matched couples among celebrities, from fashion designers to musicians and film makers.

In addition, celebrities are products that can be purchased. We cannot buy Tendulkar, though many would like to, surely, but we can buy his images (representations, to use the technical term), products and voice, for example, the cricket bats, health drinks, wall posters, stickers, comic books, all of which are marketable representations of the celebrity.

In other cases, celebrities are themselves hired out, like SRK at weddings and parties or various stars at product launches or store inaugurals where the celebrity presence is rented so as to increase the glamour quotient of the event.

We can now look at a more sophisticated way of describing what we have already discussed and, presumably, accepted. Graeme Turner defines celebrity thus:

> Celebrity is a genre of representation and a discursive effect; it is a commodity traded by the promotions, publicity, and media industries that produce these representations and their effects; and it is a cultural formation that has a social function.... (Turner 2004: 9)

What Turner is saying, in standard academic lingo, is that our preoccupation with celebrities is the *effect* of being given access to vast amounts of information, the endless circulation of images and texts, like the film magazines, talk shows, gossip, endorsements, produced by media industries. Celebrities become heroes or heroines, villains, youth icons, role models and, therefore, have a cultural function for society to look up to, emulate, be inspired by, despise or criticise.

Rojek argues that celebrity culture arose with the slow erosion of organised religion.[8] Richard Fox (2006) has demonstrated, building on John Lennon's controversial 1966 declaration that the Beatles were as famous as Jesus Christ, how religious icons, figures of belief like Jesus themselves become celebrities in contemporary culture. In the absence of Gods, society sets up alternate icons to worship and adore. The celebrity is thus born out of an absence and fills the gap left by the disappearing God. This argument should give us some cause for thought. It should not be forgotten that India produced two state chief ministers (M.G. Ramachandran and N.T. Rama Rao) who had been hugely successful, crowd-pulling film *heroes*, one of whom, N.T. Rama Rao, specialised in the mythological genre, playing assorted God-roles. These features of celebrity worship and Godliness are worth bearing in mind.

We have celebrities who function as Gods. They command our attention, we seek their successes and, of course, we would love to have their power. Here is a quick list of our contemporary Gods or Goddesses:

1. Anil Ambani and Rahul Dravid become MTV Youth Icons.
2. Kalpana Chawla and Sunita Williams (recipient of the Padma Bhushan for 2007) become models for school children. In the fortnight from 17 June to 25 June 2007, Indian newspapers carried photographs of school children praying for the safe return of Sunita Williams from her space sojourn.
3. Everybody in India, and Indians abroad, is concerned about Sachin Tendulkar's batting form.

The lives and fortunes of particular people become the subject of anxiety, pleasure and aspirations of many. Such people are celebrities.

Critics have argued that celebrity culture builds on the principle of recognition. 'Public acclaim', writes Rojek, 'answers to a deep psychological need in all of us for recognition'. 'Acclaim', he adds, 'carries the sensual pleasure of being acknowledged as an object of desire and approval' (Rojek 2001: 95). Rojek's is a well-taken point, but addresses only one side of the celebrity equation. Celebrity culture is also based on the public's *need* to recognise and be familiar with a face in an age of individualism. As stable forms of community and social interaction breakdown, such as nuclear families, floating populations and neighbours, jobs in numerous cities during a lifetime, the existence of public and recognisable figures who possess a visual familiarity become 'anchoring points in a sea of anonymous strangers' (Gilbert 2003: 89–90). Thus celebrity culture is a two-way process—*the need to be recognised on the part of the star and the need to see something familiar on the part of the public*. This also implies that celebrity is an unstable category where a person or face that loses presence in the media and, therefore in the public domain, ceases to be a celebrity. This is the irony of celebrity culture. *On the one hand she or he has to be unique and different, while on the other hand she or he must possess qualities that are recognisable enough to be valued by the society or culture as a whole.*

There is no celebrity without an audience. The audience is an integral part of the spectacle of celebrity-dom.

A celebrity becomes the model for emulation, even idealisation, because she or he is the sum total of desires and aspirations of the masses. However, this model that the celebrity becomes is not the effect of the real attributes of the person. Much of it is to do with the projection and valorisation of the attributes. It is the publicity machinery of the culture industry that informs the world that X's attributes and qualities are worthy of emulation. A celebrity's qualities are thus determined by culture industries that give significant importance to, say, Beckham's good looks or Tiger Woods' talent. These qualities then become models for others to emulate. They become dominant cultural norms such as talent, success, looks, wealth.

Celebrity Types

But are Sachin Tendulkar, M.S. Pandher and SRK the same kind of celebrities? What distinguishes Dhoni from Lalu Yadav? Or Minal Panchal from Anil Ambani? Following Chris Rojek (2001), we can isolate three types of celebrities today.

There are celebrities who achieve their fame from being part of a royal or famous family. Thus the Scindias, Rajes or the scions of the Tatas, Ambanis and Birlas are celebrities not necessarily because they have achieved great careers or done wonderful things (that they might have done so is accidental and tangential to their public fame). What Yash Birla or Aryan (SRK's son) possess is *ascribed celebrity*. We also see other kinds of ascribed celebrities, such as Pravin Mahajan who shot and killed his brother, the politician Pramod Mahajan in April 2006, whose actions are linked with the illustrious family and, therefore, acquire notoriety or fame.

Tendulkar, Sania Mirza, Vishwanathan Anand, Kalpana Chawla, Narain Karthikeyan, Mithali Raj are celebrities because of what they have *achieved*. They are recognised for extraordinary achievements in particular fields. Sports stars possess achieved celebrity status. There is a certain amount of respect here for *achieved celebrity* status, for being unusual individuals not by virtue of birth or family but because of *individual achievements*. The sports star, and here we can think of Tendulkar, Tiger Woods, Serena Williams, Lance Armstrong, Roger Federer, Michael Schumacher and Muthiah Muralitharan who as I write, has just totalled 700 test wickets, is a different order of celebrity because her or his achievement is based on work on the field. As one commentator comparing

Tendulkar to film celebrities says: 'Only the film actor draws similar obeisance, but he provides fantasy; with Tendulkar there's no need to let the imagination slip, his art is *real*' (Brijnath, undated, emphasis added). Here there is no make-up, no family connection, the person is famous for personal endeavour and achievement. This type of celebrity is significant for a number of reasons. In an earlier era there was visibility, power and fame vested with particular classes, families and people like kings and queens, landlords, saints, great warriors or philosophers. That is, celebrity status was available only to a few. With the expansion of media—beginning with photography and then films, television and now the Internet—there was a greater chance for ordinary people's achievements and assets to be visible. Thus a Sanjaya Malakar or the celebrity winners, Abhijeet Sawant and Sandeep Acharya, in the *Indian Idol* contests are possible because of the opening up of the media. Contests like *Indian Idol* also enable music manufacturers to find talent who, due to the televised contest, are already icons by the time they come to the recording studio, more easily and cheaply. Achieved celebrity status is, therefore, linked to the increased *visibility* of the achievement. More people have the chance to be or become celebrities than ever before as a result, even as the *search* for a celebrity (in say, *Indian Idol*) becomes a *promotional spectacle*. Although achieved celebrity status is also dependent upon a visibility for the sports star's achievements, in the case of the ascribed celebrity, it is hyper-visibility rather than any achievement that determines star value.

The sports hero's deeds are often *independent* of a script written for her or him. Tendulkar's cricketing performances or Roger Federer's sublime tennis are independent of their image circulated in the media. In the case of SRK or Mallika Sherawat it is the circulation of their representations that makes them celebrities. For a sports hero, therefore, it is the heroic deeds rather than the representations, though the deeds are themselves *represented* as heroic, which make them significant.

The sports star is a hero, as opposed to a mere celebrity. The celebrity, especially the film star is, according to critics, contentless, being the cumulative effect of illusions created for or about them by script-writers, action directors, make-up experts and the publicity machine (Whannel 2002: 45–6). The sports star, on the other hand, becomes a celebrity through personal effort visible for everyone to see, and *minus* any illusionary effects.

One detail illustrates what I am getting at here. Close-ups of the sports star's tense face and the strained muscle on television emphasises for us the effort, struggle and determination (for example, 15-year-old Sachin Tendulkar's bloodied mouth as he stood up unflinchingly to Waqar Younis, then the fastest bowler in the world in his debut test series, Rafael Nadal's grunts as he sent Federer scurrying across the court in the 2007 French Open final, Tiger Woods' incomprehension at missing a hole). This is *undiluted, unmediated, unscripted* effort and achievement. Opposed to this, we have the heroic fight of the film star. Sometimes, of course, the two types come together, as in the case of Tendulkar's avatar as superhero—the new super hero in a comic book series called Master Blaster from Virgin Comics (launched in 2007).[9]

A third type of celebrity would be Jahnvi or Jade Goody who become celebrities because the media sensationalises their actions like Jahnvi's suicide attempt at the Abhishek Bachchan-Aishwarya Rai wedding, Goody's alleged racial slights of Shilpa Shetty on UK's *Celebrity Big Brother*. This is *attributed celebrity*, where particular events, such as the launch of the Tata Nano in 2007–2008, suddenly become front-page news, get large-scale TV time and attract commentaries and responses from the general public.

Attributed celebrities are what Rojek identifies as 'celetoids'. These are short-term celebrities achieve their few seconds of primetime for something they have done or who they have been seen with. There was a sudden spurt of interest in Professor Loganathan and Minal Panchal, the two Indian victims of the Virginia Tech shootout in April 2007. Neither was a celebrity in the true sense of the word. Tragically, the ending of their lives gave them widespread exposure, with news reports about their alma mater, family, education and character. Photographs appeared in every major newspaper, and put a face to a person whom we would otherwise never have met or heard of. Now, months later, you would be hard put to find any mention of either in the media. So, are these two celebrities? In the true sense of the term, with little consistent or persistent media representation, they are not. However, they did appear to millions across the country in multiple media, thereby becoming temporary celebrities. Their celebrity-status was attributed through media constructions—the sad end of two Indians in the USA.

In India we have many such celetoids who appear briefly, corner media time and space, and disappear. Of the celetoids, our best examples are individuals who are caught in some scandal. Babubhai Katara, who was splashed across all the newspapers and cornered discussions about politicians and public morality, is now off the celebrity screen; Nawab Mansur Ali Khan Pataudi, who hit the headlines for poaching, became notorious. (In his case, a shift in the nature of his celebrity status when he went into hiding and finally surrendered in June 2005.) Alistair Pereira, who ran over half a dozen pavement dwellers in November 2006 and returned to P3 when the court decision came in August 2007; Telgi of the stamp paper scandal, dating back to 1995 and sentenced in 2006; and Jahnvi, who tried to commit suicide at the Abhishek Bachchan-Aishwarya Rai wedding in 2007 are celetoids. Their exploits provoke vigorous public condemnation, angry letters to newspapers, some gossip and, sooner rather than later, they disappear off the radar. There are low-key but influential figures who sometimes gain attention. Kaavya Viswanathan, the 17-year-old US-based Indian student at Harvard, started a career as a celebrity author when she was paid US$ 500,000 advance for her book *How Opal Mehta Got Kissed, Got Wild, and Got a Life*, is a celetoid. After the scandal over her plagiarism broke in *The Harvard Crimson*, she attained unparalleled notoriety and then vanished except for brief news items. *Society*, July 2007, carried a piece on phony celebrity authors where she figured prominently (Zhou 2006). Meera Gandhi and Sant Chatwal came to prominence on the front pages of the *New York Sun* for their work on Hillary Clinton's presidential campaign. *Society* magazine described them as being 'on the bandwagon for their five minutes of glory', thus making them celetoids.[10] Dileepan, the fifteen-year-old who performed a caesarean section surgery on a woman and attracted approbation, is another recent celetoid.[11] Celetoids clearly have a short shelf-life, or could even be regional in their impact and visibility.

Celetoids can also be fictional constructs, or what I term '*celefictions*'. In the West, the best example of such a celefiction from the 1990s would be Lara Croft, the video game that acquired cult following. Hannibal Lecter, the character in Thomas Harris' *Red Dragon, The Silence of the Lambs, Hannibal* and *Hannibal Rising* and popularised by no less than Anthony Hopkins in the film versions, and Neo from *The Matrix* series, are other examples of celefiction. Arguably the best known celefictions in the Western literary canon would be Hamlet and Harry Potter. The first well known celefiction, originally a character in William Shakespeare's seventeenth-century play of the same title, has become a metaphor for various moods, behaviour and contexts, with the 'to be or not to be' monologue summarising a Hamletian dilemma in everyday parlance. Harry Potter as celefiction has benefited from the biggest hype and publicity strategies the publishing world has ever known. Thus it is important to note that Potter's celebrity status is almost certainly attributable less to the character's special appeal than to the marketing mechanisms that rendered him and his contexts ('the boy who lived') famous. Celefictions, like celebrities, are brought home to us through mechanisms that render them familiar, desirable and *possessable*. Potter-magic as celefiction demonstrates the power of the media to make even a fictional character's achievements seem *heroic*—recall the debates around Potter's fate before the last volume released in July 2007. Potter demonstrates how celefictions are commodities, and how the celebrity machine sells the character as merchandise, icons and images. Potter is

a work of fiction that becomes the subject of as much speculation and longing as a real-life figure, hero or villain. Professor
Moriarty in the Holmes stories and now Voldemort would be
celefictional villains. Indeed, it is due to the power of celebrity culture that a literary character can command such power
and profits, with, again, arguably, little help from the author's
talents at sketching a character. *'Celefictionality' is the mass
'celebrification' for profit, via the construction of a mass myth
or act of imagination, the figment of one particular imagination.* The crucial difference is that celefictions have greater
staying power and reach out across greater swathes of time and
space in their stardom.

Between 2004 and 2007 in India, we can identify *Krrish*, the
film character played by Hrithik Roshan in the film of that title,
as celefiction. With the massive success of western superheroes
on Indian film screen, Spider-man, Batman and, more recently,
the Fantastic Four are now common *celefictions*. We can add
to the list, Justirisers, who seem to now occupy shelves in
every supermarket. Barbie dolls have been celefictions for ages
now and, along with super heroes, are an example of transnational commodities that have become cultural icons in diverse
cultures and localities (MacDougall 2003).

Why is it that celefictions are only *celetoids* and not *celebrities*? To begin with, many of them only have a limited existence in the media. *Krrish* masks and film tunes that became
standard components of children's costume, are not so visible
any more. We could perhaps add 'Vijay', the name Amitabh
Bachchan took in many films, playing the angry, poor young
man with the heart of gold, to the list of celefictions. Secondly,
they are always *replaced* by other fictional characters. The
Fantastic Four is edging into the space created by Spider-man.
For more enduring celefictions we can think of Garfield, Tom
and Jerry, Mickey Mouse, Harry Potter and friends, Archie and
company, and even the music and videos of pop idols or icons
like Shakira, Britney Spears or Westlife as *representations
that become celebrities*—a trend inaugurated by Madonna
where her roles became more famous than the singer. In films

we can think of James Bond. Batman, who first appeared in 1939, has stayed a cultural icon well into the twenty-first century, a feature we see associated with other superheroes as well, suggesting that humanity needs myths of a superhero at all times.[12]

What marks celefictions is that the personality or character they represent *is all there is*. That is, there is no inner or private self behind the public face. It is an unusual kind of celebrity because, as we have seen, one of the characteristics of celebrities is the general interest in the private expression behind the public face. But, in the case of celefictions, there is no private expression behind the public face because there is no person behind the character, and yet we take an undue interest in their fate, features and fortunes.[13] Celefictions, therefore, are a good example of a very postmodern condition where the image, the simulation is the reality. Thus *Krrish* is not simply *as good as* a superhero Hrithik. *Krrish is* the superhero Hrithik. The image is the reality, just as the story and character woven for us is the reality. Celefictions are commodities that build on particular types that in turn feed off and fuel imaginations. Celefictions feed off the sympathy for the orphan (Harry Potter, the 'boy who lived'), the desire for super powers (Superman), the yearning for justice (Batman) and beauty (Barbie). Thus celefictions thrive on cultural desires, fears and anxieties. Part of their attraction, despite their being fictional, is because they cater to these psychological states—a process that manufacturers and publicity agents recognise and capitalise (literally) on.

In addition to Rojek's three types, I add a fourth— the *positional celebrity*. The positional celebrity combines several features from the above four. She or he is famous and recognisable because of connections, lineage, achievement and attribution. Yet, primarily, it is her or his location that generates the media image that makes her or him a celebrity. Political or industrial celebrities are good examples of this type. Politicians have either crossed over from other domains, such as N.T. Rama Rao, M.G. Ramachandran, Vyjayanthimala from films and, more recently, Smriti Irani from television to politics. Some are descendants of connected families, like Indira Gandhi, Rahul and Maneka Gandhi, Jyotiraje Scindia, Dayanidhi Maran, Yash Birla, Mukesh and Anil Ambani, Sonia Garware. They may have earned their business or political celebrity status because of winning elections, rising through the ranks or work in their family enterprise. Yet their media presence is determined, before they have proved themselves, because of their position as Minister, Chief Minister or business tycoon. Heads of business houses, like Nooyi and Pepsico, Ratan Tata and the Tata empire, Lakshmi Mittal and the Mittal group of companies, Gates and Microsoft, and politicians are celebrities because of their position in a society or culture. Thus Amar Singh gets attention as a politician who is close to the Ambanis and the Bachchans. They imbibe the power and glamour associated with their position and hence become worthy of media attention. Even the occasional negative one, such as the media coverage of and reader responses to Mukesh Ambani's under construction, 27-storey home in Mumbai, treating it as a vulgar display of wealth in a country where thousands of people are homeless (Ahmed 2007).[14]

'Reading' Celebrity

So celebrities are the *effect* of mass-circulating media-generated text. They are *products* who can be sold and bought in the form of merchandise, fashion styles, representations from coffee mugs to wall posters or even their very presence. They are of various types, where each one of them is dependent upon the media.

Celebrity culture can be read in particular ways organised under three crucial heads: production (media-driven construction of the celebrity), text (celebrity as text, her or his representations, products and images)[15] and consumption (all of which deal with the celebrity and celebrity culture). Consumption is the audience reception of celebrity. None of these are mutually exclusive, as this book demonstrates. This book examines what I shall call *celebrity ecology*.

Celebrity ecology is the environment of a celebrity. It includes material, non-material, textual, spoken, visual, commercial and non-commercial, personal and public components working in tandem. The notion of celebrity *ecology* is built on the assumption, and emphasises the fact that the celebrity is not the effect of any one predominant element, whether media, audience, material culture, organisations or social discourses, but of all of these. Celebrity ecology looks at the environment of the celebrity *as a whole*, where the various elements in the environment interact with each other to produce the *celebrity-effect*. It gestures at the contexts in which an icon emerges, circulates and is consumed. Celebrity ecology is the setting, material nature (including physical presence, appearances and behaviour), image-making, discourses and adoration of celebrities.

The production of celebrity-dom is enabled by the value of the celebrity text (its saleability) and it is reception-consumption that determines the success of a celebrity. Celebrity ecology has five aspects:

1. Our interest in celebrity culture is an interest in *media constructions*. Celebrities must be seen as the cumulative effect of not only their achievements and lineages but of the media's representation and circulation of these achievements and lineages. This means exploring the media's projection, promotion and patronage of celebrities, and the media rituals that construct a celebrity for public consumption.

2. If celebrity culture is about media and its widespread effects, then we can study celebrities as *spectacle*. This involves studying the ways in which the media makes an aesthetic spectacle out of every small scandal and personal trait in the life of particular individuals, and thereby enables ordinary people and the audience itself to become spectacles and celebrities.

3. Since celebrity culture ensures that some people are projected as desirable or inspiring, it is linked to fashion and physical beauty cultures (that generate desirable bodies), and consumption, and we need to see *consumer culture, fashion discourses and celebrity culture as interlinked*. We need to see celebrities as linked to individual and collective desire because a celebrity is often the object of desire—in more ways than one, considering celebrity pornography—an object worth emulating.

4. We acknowledge that a certain amount of prurience is integral to the celebrity's construction and consumption. That is, *there is rarely a celebrity without a scandal*, and we need to look at what I call the 'scandalisation of public life' to deal with celebrity scandals.

5. To read celebrity culture is to look at *social processes of meaning, power and identity production*. Celebrities assert a certain amount of social, cultural and political *power*. This is not only through direct public interventions, such as Aamir Khan commenting on Narmada and Gujarat, Shabana Azmi and Arundhati Roy on various social issues, but also indirectly as well. This is achieved through a building up of a fan base or a certain relationship with the audience or public—a kind of 'parasocial relationship', a term coined by Horton and Wohl back in the 1950s (Turner 2004: 92–4). This is the relationship between, say, the fans who attacked M.S. Dhoni's house in Ranchi (March 2007) after India lost to Bangladesh in the opening match of the World Cup (2007) or the audiences who listen to Arundhati Roy at the World Social Forum (January 2004) and sign petitions when she asks them to do so. Celebrities contribute to *cultural identity*. The Indian cricket team's success becomes India's success and its failure becomes the subject of national scandal, sadness and sensation. Beauty queens winning global contests become a source of national pride. Tendulkar is a *national* asset. That is, celebrities serve a definite political and ideological

purpose, inspiring emotions of national pride, and generating images of a national triumph where the country forgets its many real problems in the wake of a sporting success.

With these assorted (perhaps ill-equipped—who knows!) navigational tools we step into Page 3, the world of celebrity culture, hoping to explore, discover and map the contours of a universe of power, glamour, looks, influence and wealth.

Notes

1. It must be made clear, right away, that it need not always be extraordinary humans who can be celebrities. The AIDS virus is, rightly, a *celebrity pathogen*, for instance, and has captured the imagination of people, from medical biologists to researchers to ordinary people, across the world. Keller (2002) notes that the gene is a celebrity in contemporary culture—her book is therefore called *The Century of the Gene*—where the genetic code, DNA, cloning and other possibilities have entranced us as nothing else has. We therefore have a *celebrity molecule*. There are disasters that have haunted our mind's eye (and the TV screen), such as the nuclear explosions over the Japanese cities, the napalmed and burning child fleeing along a road in Vietnam and the collapse of the World Trade Centre towers. These are *celebrity disasters*, whose pathos, threat and magnitude trouble us for ever afterwards. This book, however, does not deal with these other forms of celebrity culture.
2. 'We Are Not Celebrities!', *The Hindu*, Metroplus, 5 June 2007, p.1.
3. *Society*, July 2007, pp. 34–46.
4. See Anupama Chopra's hagiographic book *The King of Bollywood*, pp. 68–71, 75–8 and elsewhere.
5. *Society*, July 2007, pp. 20–3. This article was carried under the section provocatively titled 'Privileged Information', where both the information and the individual who is being studied are privileged!
6. http://film.guardian.co.uk/interview/interviewpages/0,,1837317,00.html, 4 August 2006 (downloaded on 26 January 2008).
7. Around 300 B.C., Ptolemy of Egypt minted the first coin to bear the likeness of a living ruler. Soon after, Alexander the Great minted a

coin depicting a mortal for the first time. Thus it could be argued that mass produced coins with the face of the ruler preceded photography as a medium that popularised the face of a celebrity.

8. An argument made by Rojek (2001), Chapter 2.
9. 'Sachin Tendulkar to Feature in Virgin Comics', 2 May 2007, http://www.indiaexpress.com/news/sports/cricket/20070502-0.html (downloaded on 11 June 2007).
10. *Society*, July 2007, p. 26.
11. '15-year old performs surgery in India'. www.yahoo.com, 21 June 2007 (downloaded on 21 June 2007).
12. On Batman as an enduring cultural icon see, Brooker (2000). On the superhero comic book see, among others, Nayar (2006).
13. In the same way that we discuss a Gradgrind (Dickens) or Jude (Hardy) or Hamlet (Shakespeare) as though they are real characters. We rarely say, 'Gradgrind, a fictional construct of English novelist Charles Dickens'.
14. For criticisms, see 'Mukesh Ambani's Mansion in the Air', *Mumbai Mirror*, 30 May, 2007. Available online at http://www.mumbaimirror.com/net/mmpaper.aspx?Page=article&sectid=15&contentid=20070530022210718d7460de5 (downloaded on 4 November 2007).
15. Text here is taken to mean a collection of signs, a system of representation that takes recourse to signs that acquire meaning when the reader interacts with them. Text can refer to music, visual texts such as cinema, gestures, sound and the printed text.

2

A Star is Born: Constructing Celebrity

Are you one of those who always want to know what celebrities do and how they live?

(Anusha 2007)

Celebrity culture consists of everything that is publicly available about an individual, such as images, writing, autobiography, interviews and movies. Celebrity ecology, as I have termed this, is the apparatus of representation, production, circulation and consumption of iconic figures, events and actions. Celebrity ecology consists of multiple texts in several domains, but who manufactures these texts about celebrities? Where and how do they circulate?

The celebrity, as we have seen, is the effect not only of her or his achievements but also of the media coverage of these achievements. In short, a celebrity is constructed. But how does a celebrity *become* a celebrity? Or what exactly constitutes *'celebritisation'*?

Celebritisation consists of two basic dimensions:

1. Constructing an individual as an object of desire.
2. Constructing an individual for mass consumption.

The celebrity is one whose looks, lifestyle, skills, success, behaviour or attitude become desirable qualities and set the norm for the rest of the society to emulate. She or he is also a marketable commodity in terms of the profits to be made by advertisers, movie-makers and manufacturers. In many cases, winners of contests begin to be commercially viable soon after their wins. Rachel Varghese, the nineteen-year-old winner of *Get Gorgeous 4* in 2007, was signed up by Channel V and a model management company. She has already done modelling for designers at the India Fashion Week, Delhi (Sharma 2007: 3).

A celebrity is an individual who possesses both a commercial as well as a socio-cultural value. Celebrity ecology and its apparatus seeks to control and manage the texts that emphasise these two values.

Moviemag editor Bharathi Pradhan points to the link between commercial value and celebrity lives in her column, 'Celebrity Circus'. Mani Ratnam's much-awaited *Guru* opened to fairly empty houses on a Friday (12 January 2007); on Saturday night, the Abhishek-Aishwarya Rai engagement was planned; on Sunday they exchanged rings; on Monday it hit the headlines; and 'by the end of the week *Guru* had begun to get an audience!' Pradhan zeroes in on the key element of the event by declaring it as belonging 'to the same category as a successful *promo*'.[1] Here is an illustration of the cultural and commercial value of a celebrity. A woman touted as the most beautiful in the world, a rising star belonging to the best known brand-name in Bollywood and a long-awaited film based apparently on the life of a celebrity industrialist (Dhirubhai Ambani) are all in conjunction. And the perfect example of the commercial value of a celebrity was the commercial success through the carefully timed announcement of engagement and marriage plans of the celebrity icons and the film's stars. In the *Forbes* magazine's list of the top 100 celebrities, the top ten are:

1. Oprah Winfrey
2. Tiger Woods
3. Madonna
4. The Rolling Stones
5. Brad Pitt
6. Johnny Depp

7. Elton John
8. Tom Cruise
9. Jay-Z
10. Steven Spielberg

There is *one* athlete or sports star, *one* talk show host and the rest are all entertainers. Brad Pitt is described by the magazine as a 'hunky actor, a newsstand mainstay, thanks to his hotter half and their new brood'; Steven Spielberg is 'Tinseltown's mightiest filmmaker'; Oprah is 'media queen' (Goldman et al. 2007: 82). The list says something about celebrity culture—entertainers are the largest commercial *and* cultural icons.

The dramatic denouement projected on every episode of *Indian Idol, Sa Re Ga Ma Challenge* or Star *Voice of India* is calculated to increase the tension about the potential celebrity. Newspapers carry public opinions, letters and informed analysis of trends and guesses about who the winner could be in the contest (Chougule 2007: 1).[2] All these are part of the celebrity-making process, texts that contribute to the celebrity itself.

Any celebrity-making process works to maximise the two crucial roles and values of the celebrity. Two scenarios will help us understand the dual role of the celebrity:

Scenario One:
The producer makes the film and sells it to distributors, who hire publicists to draw attention to the film. Music, television and print coverage follows. With the movie's release, money comes in for all. The profits often depend upon the star's saleability.

The sports star is paid a fee to play. The sponsors of tournaments pay the sports Boards (such as the Board of Cricket Control for India). The tournament attracts product sponsors, advertisements and promoters who pay to advertise in the grounds. The ticket sales bring in money. In cricket or (now) in tennis, ticket sales are influenced partly by the presence and form of Tendulkar and Sania Mirza.

The celebrity influences the financial economy.

Scenario Two:
The star of a successful film commands a fan following, promotes particular products, is associated with prestigious fashion houses, sets the trends in fashion, may comment on social issues or take up social work. The sports star commands a nation's respect and affection if she or he is successful and its anger if she or he does not. She or he becomes an icon for determination, hard work and talent and is often the role model for aspiring sportsmen and women.

Here the audience is the *producer*. It adopts the fashion the film star promotes or wears. Watching Tendulkar play and conquer the cricket field influences more children to take up cricket.

The celebrity influences the cultural economy.

The audience, which is the first the consumer of the celebrity, now turns producer in its own right, producing cultural artifacts, events and processes such as fashion, role models and interest in particular sports. This cultural economy is not readily quantifiable, as, for example, there is no direct sign of their *financial* role, but it exists nevertheless.

The cultural economy in turn fuels the financial scenario. More fashion leads to greater consumption and therefore production, more sports means more organisations, sponsors and product manufacture. This could throw up more celebrities. M.S. Dhoni, now a national youth icon, has stated on record of how he grew up watching Tendulkar play.[3] Furthermore, all sport is now *media sport*. Men's magazines, television, print and tabloid journalism, advertising and websites have enabled sports events and players to reach wider audiences. It has also enabled players to be recognised by large numbers, with many emerging as stars. 'Star Sports', argues Rohit Brijnath writing for Living Media, 'had much to do with the celebrity status of Tendulkar':

A young new-age hero needed his medium and in TV he found it. In a distracted world of the '90s, our lives

cluttered by information, demonstration of genius was important. To spread his gospel further and quicker, Sachin required
pictures...

In 1993, as England toured, and his batting began to find mature
flourish, India embraced Star Sports. Every stroke was explained,
every stroke shown, from the sides, in front, on top, behind,
the mechanics of his brilliance on continuous display. And
through the years as he did it again and again and again, we were
there with him. (Brijnath, undated)

The comment sums up the link between talent, media sport
and celebrity culture. David Beckham, arguably the most
photographed and recognisable sports star of the twentieth
century (Michael Jordan, Tiger Woods, and now Roger
Federer, come close), is, at least partly, the creation of a media
whose interest in Beckham's career and personal life borders
on obsession. These stars, while commanding national, ethnic,
racial and community loyalty, fervour and admiration—the
cultural capital accruing to celebrity—is also a high profile
fashion, advertising or media icon generating profits through
increased sales of products.

Tendulkar is not only India's national hero, but also represents a marketable commodity. Listed in *India Today*'s '100
People who Shaped India', Tendulkar is even described as a
God in a country where an 'absence of heroes enhances his
appeal' (Brijnath, undated). Amitabh Bachchan is not only
a huge commercial draw, but also represents the best of
Bollywood for the world to recognise. Aamir Khan with *Lagaan*
took us to the Oscars, but he also assures us that billion-dollar,
profit-making Coca-Cola is a safe drink.

These celebrities provide pleasure as well as economic profit.
They are commodities because they are sold for the public to
consume and attain pleasure through the process of consumption. Consumption here is not simply the viewing of the latest
movie of the star but includes the consumption of news about
the star, following her or his career, purchase of products
endorsed by her/him. We consume their glamour, and crave
for more. We take an interest in their personal lives, and are

eager to know more. We believe they possess certain credibility, and therefore buy the product they create or endorse. As Ellis Cashmore tells us, 'consumers thrill to the sight and sound of celebrities, not because they're dupes, suckers, airheads, or simpletons, but because they have become willing accomplices in the enterprise' (Cashmore 2006: 266).

The celebrity is thus situated at the intersection of, and is the effect of, the interaction between the financial and cultural economy. The *ecology* of the celebrity is this intersection.

Desiring Celebrity

A celebrity is what is desired and appears desirable. This desirability rests not simply in the looks or achievements of a person, but the media's *validation, praise* and *reproduction* of their achievements and looks. In the media, we see regular photographs of celebrity events where individuals we have come to see as celebrities perform certain roles. During every cricket tour or season, we are given details of Tendulkar's batting record over the years. This media coverage shows why a celebrity is a celebrity and why he or she does what we would like to do, or ought to do: to excel. This is especially true of achieved celebrity where the success of an individual person is reproduced endlessly. Tendulkar is always the 'master blaster' and Dravid is always 'The Wall', epithets that circulate for us to immediately recognise them as special. This is the desirability production of a celebrity. It is media-exemplification, where the media constructs individuals as exemplars, the best examples of humanity, a field of expertise or a culture, to be emulated and worshipped. In the case of film stars, an additional dimension to desire is visible, namely, attractiveness. Whether it is the machismo image of John Abraham and his bike in the Castrol advertisement campaign or the shots of Abhishek-Aishwarya Rai at Cannes 2007, we are given images of perfect bodies and sensational looks that are groomed and fit. These represent what we want to be or become.

The media generates consumable celebrities and renders them as products to be bought and exchanged. A celebrity is a piece of property that is highly valuable, marketable and visible. A celebrity generates income, she or he is an asset and an economic source. A celebrity is a commodity that is manufactured and marketed by industries. Thus SRK—'the most famous man on earth' as the current tagline goes—is a *brand* that can sell a film or a product. Part of the process of selling 'brand SRK' is to ensure a surplus of information about, and images of SRK in the media, such as biographies, posters, song sequences on TV and interviews. The media industry ensures that SRK is never out of our attention or focus.

Information, marketing and media industries produce the celebrity for consumption. Thus different kinds of industries merge to produce the *celebrity-effect* even as the celebrity affects different fields. In fact, one of the key features of the celebrity is this ability to occupy different fields, to have different fields converging upon them.

However, not all celebrities are of the same type. David Marshall proposes a scheme of identification that helps us distinguish *between* celebrities (Marshall 1997: 185–199). Film stars generate what he terms *auratic identification*. SRK, Big B, Julia Roberts and Keira Knightley are celebrities because, even though they are familiar, there remains a certain distance between them and the audience. As an aura develops around them, their looks, wealth, lifestyle, all emphasised and circulated through the media, *distance* them from us. It is in their very difference and distance from us that they come into existence as celebrities.

On the other hand, Aman Verma and Smriti Irani are television personalities who have become celebrities because they are *like us*. In such cases we have a *sympathetic identification* with them. It is in their *familiarity* of character and situations that their recognisability and star value exist. It could very well explain their success and appeal in soap operas.

Finally, Marshall proposes an *associative identification* with pop stars, where the lyrics, presentation and styles become part of a collective process, with masses of people joining in to wave, sing along and participate.

I add a fourth category of identification to Marshall's classification. In the case of sports celebrities like Dhoni or Tiger Woods, we have a different order of identification that is similar to but is more than Marshall's associative one. They represent effort, determination and attendant success that inspire others to *follow* them. The relationship of Dhoni with his fans could best be described as *mimetic identification* where his heroics on the cricket field are seen as *worthy of emulation.*[4]

Tendulkar rises from a middle-class background and Tiger Woods' success as an African American in a society notorious for its racism is not only a source of cultural identity but also constitute success stories that youngsters can be brought up on. Jesse Owens is arguably the first such African American celebrity to effect a *mimetic* identification among the coloured people. Children want to *be* Tendulkar ('har ghar mein Sachin', as the biscuit advertisement goes). This is mimetic identification with a celebrity who possesses qualities that inspire others to work harder for success. What we get here is a sports *hero* more than a mere sports celebrity or sports star. These kinds of identifications are media-generated and controlled, and are best studied as the consequences of media rituals.

Media Rituals

Media rituals in celebrity ecology are actions organised around the media's various functions. This can be ritual *viewing* of particular television programmes or website *visits*, how people *speak of* appearing in the media, and our own heightened *attention* in the presence of a media celebrity or a media person, such as a newspaper reporter. Media rituals enable social cohesion and reinforce social myths and ideologies. Tendulkar becomes a *national* hero through sustained media representations, such as news reports, philanthropic work telecast live, biographical accounts on TV, birthday greetings and mentions in newspapers, for us to follow.[5] Media rituals help structure meanings and provide frames within which particular ideologies work.[6] For example, in the case given above, Tendulkar unifies, however temporarily or superficially, all Indians as his fans. As I write, he has scored his 39th Test century in Australia, January 2008 and we are treated to the astonishing sight of a crowd of toughened sports lovers give a standing ovation to the acknowledged genius of the cricket field. In a sense, national identity is a Tendulkar-effect achieved *through* media rituals. Or, in the case of national figures like Gandhi, Ambedkar or Nehru, anniversaries and birth centenaries become spaces of ritual honouring, memorial services and prayers, and even treating these days as national holidays, all of which contribute to their stature as national, that is, pan-*Indian*.

Why this emphasis on media at all? There are two reasons. First, as already noted, celebrities are constructed through the media's representations. Media is perhaps the single-most important element in celebrity ecology. Second, media institutions generate enormous *symbolic* power. This may not be the power to alter social inequalities (though media reports have enabled courts to take *suo moto* cognisance of the events and the act), but power to embarrass the wealthy, showcase good qualities and courage. It adds a certain social value to people. This is symbolic power. Media informs and drives the celebrity industries, which are themselves made up of diverse components. These include:

1. the film and television or *entertainment* industry (Bollywood, Balaji Telefilms, MTV),
2. newspapers and magazines or *information and communication* (which might also have film and television) industry (*Filmfare*, *Star and Style*, the newspapers),
3. publicists or *marketing* industry (advertising, promotion companies, publicity agents),

4. fashion makers, hair and clothes stylists or *fashion industry* (Manish Malhotra, Rohit Bal, Habib's hair styling salons)
5. trainers, fitness experts, dance, music or theatre coaching or *training* industry (Shiamak Davar's dance school, Saroj Khan, National School of Drama)
6. authors like P. Sainath, Amartya Sen or Ramachandra Guha whose journalism constitutes a major *literary* industry in metropolises.

We could say that the celebrity effect is produced by the combined and complementary efforts of these components, like *entertainment, information and communication, marketing, fashion, training, literature,* of the celebrity industries. It is the convergence of the practices of these industries, all informed, disseminated and even controlled by the mass media that generates the celebrity.

Rituals are *formal* acts set in social contexts, and they communicate and legitimise social values in specialised constructed contexts. There exists a ritual space of the media made of an interlocking mass of practices (Couldry 2003: 13). This mass of practices includes diverse things, such as setting, actions, conversations, viewing, camera movements, voice-overs, primetime viewing, telecast rights, advertisements, promos, endorsements, sponsorship, all of which contribute to the transformation of the site or person into a celebrity space. The media's ritual space consists of varied elements and practices. The setting at Rajghat on Gandhi Jayanti, the solemn procession, the speeches, the floral tributes, the prayers and the moments of silence by the audience serve to transform the grave into a celebrity site through such ceremonial *acts*, where each combines with the rest to produce a celebrity-effect of mourning and memory. In the case of a TV show, *Koffee with Karan*, the *setting* of the studio with its green motif, the location of the participants on sofas rather than formal chairs, Karan Johar sipping coffee before the guest arrives are spatial arrangements that transform the space into a ritualistic one.

In the case of *Indian Idol*, it is the hosts' reference to the story so far in her or his opening *speech* that increases the dramatic tension before the contest of the day. In the case of films, audience *responses* telecast on TV ensure the film's significant status at least on the opening day. These acts, speech, setting, response are media's ritual acts central to celebrity culture. In each case the ritual includes entertainment, fashion, information and marketing aspects. Media rituals can be of various types and formats.

Contests

If not for 'Indian Idol', I would have been another neighbour-hood boy in a nondescript Mulund colony of Mumbai ... People already recognise me on the street, I have money in my bank account that I couldn't dream of six months back.

— Abhijeet Sawant, winner, *Indian Idol 2*

I have been a recognised face in local functions but my dream was to reach Bollywood. Now, everyone has come to know me.

— Sunil Pal, winner, *Great Indian Laughter Challenge*
(Pisharoty 2005)

The two comments capture the popularity and the celebrity-making potential of Reality TV and contests. It therefore comes as no surprise when we hear that for the new round of *American Idol* (season 7), news agencies in July-August 2007 reported thousands of people (12,000 in some cases) waiting through the night to be first in line for the audition.[7]

Television talent contests are extraordinarily popular, heavily subscribed to, judging by the advertisements and the TRPs, media events. Glamorous, choreographed, live and therefore *real*, these contests are *rituals* of competition. Television contests are media rituals where the distinctions between the two principal sets of actors are emphasised—

1. the *participants* and *the audience* (who vote and decide the fate of the participants),
2. the *participants* and the *judges* (who finally adjudicate).

This set of distinctions and categories is the *first frame of the actual ritual or contest where the immediate actors are located*. In addition, there is a larger frame of the social norms in which the contest itself is located. If the first frame is the scene of the action, *the second frame is the set of cultural values in and through which the audience looks at the participants and evaluates the contest and winner*. The first frame is the *setting* and action, the second is the *reception* of the events as informed by social codes and norms. The second frame is the society or culture's belief system that works while we interpret the ritual or contest. The belief system or set of values gets embodied or ritualised in the contest. Thus belief systems like 'hard work pays' is what gets ritualised in *Indian Idol*. The contest reinstates this belief system through the structure of the contest where the actions separate the winner (who has worked hard) from the loser.

The contest is a media-driven ritual in which an ordinary person is transformed into a success and into a celebrity, because she or he has moved from the space of the contest into the space of the social beliefs that receives the contest. She or he is a celebrity because the mediated ritual shows how she or he is different from the others and reinforces the belief that 'hard work pays: witness X on *Indian Idol*'.

The ritual of the contest legitimises the underlying social value of talent, of some people being better than others. In a sense, the ritual space of contests like *Indian Idol* reinforces the inequalities among people. Contests like *Indian Idol* constitute a *narrative of difference* where we see select individuals rise from the crowd and become celebrities. We watch the process through which individuals rise above the ordinary on the way to being celebrities. Flashbacks in *Indian Idol*, to show the path by which the contestant has reached the advanced rounds are also part of this narrative. On 8 September 2007, they telecast clips of the reception accorded to the contestants when they went back home after four months on *Indian Idol*. There were shots of massive crowds lining the streets, meeting the famous and the powerful in their state, hysterical college girls cheering, and even a shot of one of the contestants, Emon, lying in his mother's lap. All this served to generate a certain amount of *affective* or emotional attachment of the audience to the ordinary boy who has come this far on the route to stardom.

A diagrammatic representation of the sequence of the ritual would be something like this:

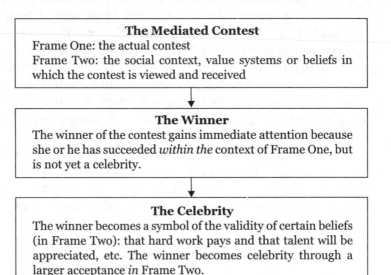

The Mediated Contest
Frame One: the actual contest
Frame Two: the social context, value systems or beliefs in which the contest is viewed and received

The Winner
The winner of the contest gains immediate attention because she or he has succeeded *within the* context of Frame One, but is not yet a celebrity.

The Celebrity
The winner becomes a symbol of the validity of certain beliefs (in Frame Two): that hard work pays and that talent will be appreciated, etc. The winner becomes celebrity through a larger acceptance *in* Frame Two.

Contests treat difference and unequal talents as natural and some talents as exceedingly desirable. We are trained to accept this fact, and it is in this acceptance that celebrities are constructed. What we watch joyfully is, in Charles Fairchild's description of *Australian Idol*, the 'narrative of aesthetic order in the face of a perceived industrial chaos', where there are many pretenders, brands, music manufacturers and only a few who are really talented (Fairchild 2007: 360).

There is a touch of the soap opera in the talent contests. Shots of the emotional outbursts of the contestants, interviews with family members and the excessive enthusiasm exhibited by the contestants lend an air of *theatricality* on *Indian Idol*. We see winners fall down on the ground and scream or we see losers start crying. The appropriate touch of so-called irrational behaviour lends the contest a human touch and to show the other side of the competition. The contest merges here with the talk show where a person admits to her or his deep fears and anxieties to an audience or seeks advice from the expert or host or the audience. It also merges with the soap opera or cinema with its moments of drama.

This theatricality and exhibition of private feelings is also part of the celebrity cult. The audience responds to the show of emotions. If once celebrities were produced in specialised fields, Reality TV ensures that celebrities are those who succeed in multiple domains—singers are also performers. *Indian Idol* judges underscore this when they praise a participant's per-formance, even as they mourn their poor singing. Performance here clearly means stage presence and actions. They occupy the domains of drama, contest, fashion and mediagenic looks. The line between authenticity and inauthenticity that gets blurred in such exhibitions is part of the media ritual. The contestant is putting on an act of enormous affection for a fellow competitor or the cheery good lucks to a rival.

To an increasing degree, there is an emphasis on being *talented, popular* and *acceptable,* and Reality Television and contests are media rituals that legitimise these *desirable values.* Here an interesting element creeps into the narrative of *Indian Idol.* It is not enough for Emon or Prashant (as I write in early September 2007, two of the final three, along with Amit) to possess looks or talent. They must be *willing* to listen to the judges and industry and alter themselves according to the suggestions made. Every judge offers tips on improving their voice or singing abilities or chastises them, Anu Malik in particular in *Indian Idol 3*, for wasting their talent or committing mistakes, and the contestants frequently acknowledging the help they received in the form of such tips. Thus *Idol* suggests that talent has to be groomed, and this is where the contest comes in. Its narrative suggests that the contest, which becomes a metonym for the music and entertainment industry itself, *is already grooming raw talents into performing better* so that the performer becomes more attractive and therefore more marketable. Thus the process of winning the contest is also the process of grooming, of getting ready to be a part of the industry.

The carefully choreographed emotional performances—an ecology in which a new form of life, the celebrity emerges and flourishes—of the winners, the screaming crowds, the jury comments, the SMS voting are all components of the ritual space of the media where specific values and qualities are reinforced. Celebrities are those who possess the desirable values and talents as these are defined and determined by the judges and the audience. Talent searches that throw up celebrities are basically *rituals of differentiation*, that is, of separating people on the basis of so-called talents.

Curiously, contests like *Indian Idol*, spread over several months, renders the celebrity *unstable*. It is never enough for a contestant to perform well once. With each round, and dwindling numbers, the stakes are higher, and the audience or the viewer is continually asked to ensure that X or Y makes it to the next round. Even as the contestants are on their way to becoming pop stars or celebrities, their identity *as* successful icons or talents is constantly called into question. Icons like Sunidhi Chauhan, who was also discovered and groomed through such a contest, have much to do with this. This is the drama of the unstable celebrity cult.

Celebrities such as Sanjaya Malakar (the *American Idol 6* contestant) or the winners of *Indian Idol* are thus the effect of the media endorsing particular talents. The media not only creates celebrities but also *legitimises* specific values. This is the symbolic power of the media—a power that organises the media ritual of contests, judging, winning and rewards and is not readily quantifiable but confers prestige and acclaim. Former winners of contests publicising the contests—also, now, a media ritual—ask more people to participate, while ensuring that such contests and rituals continue. Promoting the *Filmfare* awards 2007, Amitabh Bachchan and Karan Johar appeared on television urging us to watch this black tie, exclusive event. These are media rituals that possess the symbolic power of organising audiences, of getting people to slot the television viewing into their daily life.

What such contests do is to construct celebrities via an ideology of merit. Contests are an excellent example of media rituals that seek to implement a meritocracy, where any individual who has a particular talent and who can present it well can rise above the rest. In a nation where the demand for equality, especially equality of access and a more effective and responsive democracy that is now strident, contests only reinforce inequality. On the one hand, affirmative action, court orders and legislation seeks to make society less differentiated and more democratic by enabling the less privileged and talented equal access to education, wealth and power. On the other hand, the contests focus on difference and unequal talent in order to capitalise upon certain virtues. Contests move people into the capitalist competitive mode in an era when the state itself seeks democratisation and equality. They become parallel stages and forums, other than the state, where merit is evaluated and rewarded even as the state seeks to link merit with access to facilities. This is a carefully orchestrated shift where talents are evaluated, endorsed, rewarded and then sold, a process I term *meritocratic capitalism*, which focusses on *individual* enterprise, talent, effort and success. Meritocratic capitalism with its emphasis on the individual is, ironically, possible only through the careful manipulation of the ecology in which such contests are held. It is thus an artificial environment where particular values are highlighted and evaluated.

In and Out

Media's ritual categories propagate the cult of in-ness that it generates and perpetuates. The media constructs difference on the basis of what is in and what is *not* in. Columns on what is fashionable this season determine clothing, consumption and photogenic appearance. P3 supplements that focus on what particular celebrities are wearing are media rituals where difference is constructed. What is *in* is differentiated from what is not *in*. This difference is then, through repeated usage and through several representations—particular kinds of clothes or accessories sported by celebrities on TV or on P3—naturalised. If contests serve as media rituals of meritocratic differentiation and therefore of social hierarchy, then media representations of fashion also constitute rituals of social ranking and hierarchy. In all these cases, the rituals *market* specific looks, skills and appeal, the meritocratic capitalism where everything can be represented for sales and marketed as values, and purchased as commodities.

Media rituals increasingly include profile management. Celebrities, especially from the world of film or sports, are called in to inaugurate showrooms, launch products or distribute awards. Linked closely with celebrity product endorsement, this media ritual of stars opening showrooms and malls constitute rituals of desirability. The product or space is a desirable one through its use or demonstration by the celebrity. The fact that the celebrity is paid large amounts of money to inaugurate is not showcased in the media representation of the event. This ritual category is about recognition. The celebrity recognises a product when she or he launches it, or appreciates a talent or luck when awarding a prize to a contest winner. Thus Bollywood stars, from Sunjay Dutt to Riteish Deshmukh, seem to be crucial to *Indian Idol*. In fact, Bollywood stars seem to be crucial presences at any contest or TV programme.

The profile management of the product or mall is the construction of desirable spaces or products through a public ritual of launches, inaugurations and ceremonies, and is central to meritocratic capitalism. It sets the space apart from other stores or products through the association of the celebrity. Once again, it is the ideology of differentiation that underlies the media ritual of launches.

A notable feature of media rituals is the link between celebrity and sexuality. Celebrities use strategies of *sexualised* visual culture, which does not always mean erotic or pornographic. Their portrayals in magazines as diverse as *People* and *Filmfare*, on their official websites and fansites and of course in promotional material are often sexualised and eroticised to induce and enhance their appeal. Jacqueline Lambiase (2003) has developed a useful typology of the sexualised celebrity. Irfan Khan, Esha Deol, Rahul Dravid, Saif Ali Khan sell products in which their role as celebrities is not only hinged upon sex appeal but also on recognisability. These are *decorative roles* where their clothing, attitudes, actions and expression is routine, even though these are all carefully planned to enhance their attractiveness. There is no celebrity visual culture that does not seek to underscore attractiveness or desirability, though in the decorative role this is not so much the emphasis. The traditional category of *sexualised celebrity*, according to Lambiase, work on stereotypes. We see it in the *feminised* Hema Malini advertising for healthy homes (water purifiers) and the *machismo* John Abraham for bikes. The third type is the *progressive role*—an attempt to use sexualised celebrities for suggesting a different political or social structure. Abhishek Bachchan doing domestic chores that reverses the stereotyped gender roles in the home is an example. Lambiase's study shows how celebrity websites, both official and fan sites, often use suggestive clothing, which could include appearing in a partially nude state as in the case of J-Lo, Shakira, Britney Spears and Jennifer Aniston, even on their official sites.[8] These codes of sexualised appearance are performances that enhance the celebrity's appeal because they are associated with the celebrity as part of their *brand* image. In other words, sexuality is part of the celebrity's trademark and is therefore integral to their construction.

Media Sites

Media rituals are located not necessarily in television studios and stage shows—though these constitute the most widely disseminated media rituals. There are sites—Nick Couldry terms these as media sites—where such rituals take place (Couldry 2003: 51–2).

On the route to my place of work, the University of Hyderabad, (Hyderabad), I pass, first, an old fortress-like place on a small hillock called Nanalnagar and second, the Andhra Pradesh sports complex-stadium at a place called Gachibowli. The first is a rather tumble-down quasi-Gothic structure now painted, inexplicably, a hideous white. The second is an ultra-modern facility, marked specifically by a wide sweep of concrete road that is, surprisingly for an Indian road, still intact. A routine sight at these places is a camera crew in action. There is, as expected, a massive crowd of onlookers surrounding the action. This is a media site, where people from the non-media world cross into the media world, at least temporarily. It is the site of media rituals.

Media sites include great spots such as the Taj (Edensor 1998). They also, paradoxically, include places of disaster where survivors or witnesses appear as celetoids and whose presence is ephemeral and rarely repeated or interviews on television. After the Mecca Masjid blasts in Hyderabad in May 2007 and the Lumbini Park-Gokul eatery blasts in August 2007, we were treated to the same shots and interviews with the witnesses and who thereafter disappeared from our screens and lives. Media sites are also those where media persons accost passers-by for their opinions. *MTV Bakra* and Pogo's *Just for Laughs: Gags* are both instances of such sites where everyday street life and the passer-by are on camera, a technique that has come to be called candid camera after the American TV series.[9] There are media sites where winners of contests get to shake hands with Tendulkar or dine with a celebrity. Talk shows or shows such as *KBC* also constitute media sites when the audience is called upon to express an opinion or make a comment, or when

SRK addresses the family of the contestant seated in the gallery audience. Inauguration of restaurants, malls, shopping areas often catch shoppers or consumers on camera. These are also media sites where a certain ritual, such as a shopper smiling self-consciously at the camera, is performed.

Media rituals are stage-managed by celebrity managers and PR personnel, ensuring that the icon stays within the public eye through carefully chosen presencing. Media rituals offer the consumer what she or he wants, but work to *sustain* this desire. Rituals are, as theorists of performance have argued, physiological, where facial expression, physical presence, sounds and gestures as well as colour, smell, sounds and sights are all an integral part of this ritual.[10] In celebrity media rituals the physical presence of the *event* or celebrity *body* is central and the *celebrity-effect* is the apparent absence of mediation like editing or voice-overs). The large gatherings at store openings or star functions constitute a ritual of *immediacy*, where the fans seek to get as close to the celebrity without mediation. Ironically, it is crowd control and the deliberate *distancing* of the star in the form of security that emphasises the reality of the celebrity. This simultaneous distancing and immediacy is a part of the media ritual that underscores the celebrity-hood.

Media Events

An important media ritual in celebrity ecology is the public event. Dayan and Katz termed media events as those televised or broadcast public ceremonies that occur in a capital or the centre of the society or nation (Dayan and Katz 1992). This media event is a *real* event, not one engineered by the media. What is important is that this media event interrupts regular telecast. That is, these events are not part of the everyday television viewing experience. The Independence and Republic Day parades in New Delhi, the telecast of swearing in of governments and sports meets are a few examples. The nation *as a whole* is called upon to participate in the ritual or ceremony via the live telecasts, thus making it a participatory spectacle. The celebrity event, by virtue not only of its components of political or sports celebrities, but also by its rarity and august formal arrangements, is a media ritual whereby the entity of India is circulated and shared by all viewers across the territory. The media event focalises *as* the centre of Indianness like the Rashtrapati Bhawan, Red Fort (New Delhi), with the space and the location of the event.

It is important to note that these events acquire celebrity status mainly through the power of the media. As we have seen in the introductory chapter, celebrities are possible through the media's circulation of images. Events such as the Republic Day parade are celebrity events, as are the guests at the parade, mainly because the telecast takes it to the people. It is, therefore, a *mediated* event (by mediated I mean both, circulated in the media, but also influenced, interfered with, altered by the media. I use the term 'mediated' to gesture at the role of the media/medium but also the consequence of mediation). We shall return to the spectacular nature of the event later.

Celebrity Locales

The media is also influential in transforming specific sites into celebrity locales. These are not simply media sites, but rather, they are places with a certain aura, affective power and prestige around them.

Locations where particular films have been made, such as the Ramnagar village near Bangalore where Bollywood's most famous film *Sholay* was shot or Kunaria village near Bhuj in Gujarat's Kutch district where *Lagaan* was shot, are locales that have become famous as the setting of popular and successful films, and the subject of media attention for these same films.[11]

More recently, sites of what Nick Couldry terms media pilgrimages—visits to places made famous by media—include film sets and film industry tours (Couldry 2003: 75–94). Ramoji Film City in Hyderabad is now a major tourist attraction and could be used as an example of such a celebrity locale where celebrity events—films—have been made. These visits are also media rituals, showcasing the power of celebrities and acknowledging the social hierarchies within which we live (famous/not-famous, ordinary/extraordinary, mediagenic/ non-mediagenic).

Memorials like Rajghat for instance are also celebrity locales and media-pilgrimage sites. The birth or death anniversaries of Indira Gandhi, Jaya Prakash Narayan, Mahatma Gandhi and others are focussed on a mediated spectacle of homage at these sites.[12] Statues where political parties and leaders come to pay homage on anniversaries are also celebrity sites.

What such media pilgrimages and location-shooting spectacles ensure is the celebrity-hood of celebrities. Focus on the star shooting at the location surrounded by gaping onlookers, enables us to understand the symbolic value of the individual in society. Here we can see the flesh-and-blood person who commands so much symbolic and commercial value, demonstrating exactly why she or he is so unique. This viewing is also mediated, especially in India, by the film posters, gossip magazines and the economy of the film industry.

Reality TV

Bigg Boss, launched in November 2006, presented the Indian equivalent of the phenomenally successful, *Big Brother* (UK). Starting with 13 celebrities in a house, on camera 24×7, *Bigg Boss* promised a revolution in entertainment. Here is what Set India said:

> Come November 3, 2006 and Indian television will catapult into a new era of *entertainment*. While reality shows add spice to people's lives, daily soaps continue to be the staple diet here in India. The launch of *Bigg Boss* brings you the unique combination of *reality and real unscripted drama* as 13 celebrities vie with each other

to survive in the Bigg Boss house. A *reality-based soap* that is a pot-boiler of drama & emotions, that forms the main ingredient of popular soaps, in fact further this is *all real and unscripted making for pure drama*. Premiering on November 3rd, *Bigg Boss* is a daily from Monday to Thursday, at 10.00 p.m and on Fridays, the eviction episode will play out at 9.00 p.m.[13]

What exactly does a reality show mean for celebrity culture? In the case of *Bigg Boss*, it is important to note that most of the participants are celebrities, arguably minor, but with some degree of public recognition already available to them. The show adds an additional layer to this recognition, but with a difference. The structure and nature of television reality shows demonstrates this reification of the celebrity.

Set India clearly promotes *Bigg Boss* as *entertainment*. It is 'real and unscripted drama' (the phrase occurs twice) and a 'reality-based soap'. Reality TV is both artificial entertainment and human reality for mass consumption. It is supposedly *unmediated* reality. The use of terms like drama and soap suggests the addition of a quality that reality might otherwise lack.

In the case of UK's *Big Brother* or *Castaway*, the ordinariness of the participants made it seem more real. Here are people like you and me, in this house under 24×7 surveillance. The social reality of people discovering each other, building relationships under the watchful eye of the camera was intended as a new degree of *realism*.

It is the sense of liveness that the show's producers seek to capitalise on. Reality TV mixes popular entertainment with real life (Ouellette and Murray 2004: 2). Indeed, real life itself becomes a marketable commodity and the protagonist of the show becomes *first* an actor and *second* a celebrity. Ironically, what Reality TV does is to emphasise the centrality of the media. The participants *know* they are on camera and live, that is, the show's claim to reality or liveness is a mediated construction. What Reality TV does is to call our attention to the *process of representation*—filming. If, as George Orwell's terrifying vision of the future, *Nineteen Eighty Four*, predicts, you an otherwise ordinary person, are always being watched, Reality TV makes this possible.

The appeal of Reality TV lies in the fact that perfectly unremarkable people suddenly become remarkable, with commercial and cultural benefits accruing to them over time, thanks to the media.

Reality TV is thus situated somewhere between carefully crafted fiction and reality. *Survivor*, the popular reality game across the world (telecast on AXN), becomes popular because it is a *hybrid genre of games, adventure and drama* with an essential unpredictability woven into the script (Haralovich and Trosset 2004: 76–7). Whether the player survives or not is dependent upon the abilities and the context. The audience is invited to predict who would be voted off the show. This prediction is based on what we have seen of players so far and our general frames of interpreting ability and reality. It is, however, also based on a scepticism about the amount of information that the audience gets. The *edited* version is what is telecast. It is this that lends an air of drama to the programme. In cases such as the controversial *Kid Nation* (CBS, launched in the USA in September 2007), equivalent of *Big Brother*, children were left inside a house for 40 days without parental supervision. One drank bleach and another received a burn while trying to cook. Drama and horrific reality combine in what is being called the 'Lord of the Flies for the Reality TV generation' (Glaister 2007: 11). In fact, the horrific reality of burnt and damaged children is the drama of *Kid Nation*.

Reality TV is situated along a continuum with other mechanisms of filming and surveillance. Camcorders and cell phone cameras allow anyone to become a filmmaker. Anyone can film anyone and anything, and transmit it to television companies, newspapers or even upload it on publicised blogs. *Bigg Boss* is to be seen alongside the live recording genres such as the cell phone or camcorder film of abuse inside Abu Ghraib prison or the execution of Saddam Hussain, filmed accidentally, with no producer or script writer or director issuing orders. Also, one can usefully compare it with news reportage, using as an example the telecast of the Rajasthan violence of June 2007 when the Gujjar community rioted.

Reality TV underscores the process of filmmaking by *publicising the filming of reality* in such a way that the reality attains a marketable value—what Laurie Ouellette and Susan Murray have termed 'the commercialization of the real' (Ouellette and Murray 2004: 7). Since it is being telecast, it stands to reason that somebody in the production department can cut off transmission whenever she or he feels like it. It has the *potential* of being interrupted because it is being monitored. Thus, even live TV is *reality constructed for consumption*. Liveness is mediated not only through the self-conscious references to being on camera but also through the positing of an audience, 'who wants to watch *Bigg Boss*'? By asking viewers to vote for evictions, it ensures that the audience becomes a part of the process of mediating the real lives of the people inside the house. Reality TV's phone-in or SMS voting involves us with the 'characters' inside the house. This interactivity is a democratisation of the world of television. We now have a role to play in deciding who we would like to watch in *Bigg Boss* or we can contribute to the *Indian Idol* participant's celebrity status or loss.

Likewise, phone-ins, audience reports and sound bytes from real people not on the show adds a degree of liveness and reality. Live chat on websites and phone sites indicate this in their very use of the term, 'live'. My point is that *telephonic and other links to real people in the course of a programme suggests, implicitly, the liveness of the programme itself*. People phoning in during a programme, a feature of both television and radio, suggests that the programme is real too, since it is taking calls from real people. What is interesting about *Bigg Boss* is the nature of the people inside, like the minor celebrities, as we have noted earlier. If other Reality TV turns ordinary people into celebrities, what does *Bigg Boss* do?

Fading stars, like Deepak Parasher or Rahul Roy or current celebrities like Rakhi Sawant, develop an ordinariness on Reality TV that is central to celebrity culture. We have noted that celebrity culture thrives on the breakdown of barriers between private lives and public faces: a person becomes a celebrity when the society begins to take a greater interest in the lives behind the public face. *Bigg Boss* is located at this very point. By providing Rakhi Sawant live, without make-up, as the write-up insists, it ironically accentuates her celebrity status. We will watch Rakhi Sawant despite the absence of make-up. It is this ordinarising that adds to the glamour of a celebrity. At this point it is useful to recall photographs of Brad Pitt and Angelina Jolie riding autorickshaws or walking in Mumbai on their 2006 visit to India and headlines like 'Spotted: Brangelina in Mumbai'.[14] Stars come down to earth?

Reality TV exchanges one kind of surveillance for another, while altering the nature of the object under surveillance. *Bigg Boss* was born at a time when supermarkets and stores in India introduced the store cameras (CCTVs) for surveillance. In both contexts a social reality is being recorded endlessly. What *Bigg Boss* does is to extend surveillance, assuming that it is natural to be under surveillance, to have a camera filming one's private life. What it claims, as the write-up shows, is that reality is what is revealed under surveillance, even when the participants are aware that they are on camera.

Self-Disclosure

Talk shows, with ordinary people and celebrities, are commonplace on television. *Koffee with Karan*, *Rendezvous with Simi Garewal* and *NextGen* by Shweta Nanda are popular, though they do not (yet) have the cult status of the Oprah Winfrey show.[15] Blogs, especially those that are identified as *private*, serve as web equivalents of the talk show's confessional or self-disclosure mode because they publish for general consumption what is essentially a *cyber-diary*. In the talk show, the interlocutor elicits acts of self-disclosure. In the private blog, also telecast or published on the Internet, the audience can access an individual's private diary.[16] Like talk shows, blogs constitute a social activity because they are potentially open to anonymous readers. Blogs can become celebrities in their own right when more and more people begin to access them.

Madhuri Dixit, making a comeback to Bollywood, was the celebrity on the talk show *Koffee with Karan*. In a shift of formats, the show turned to her former co-stars Anil Kapoor, Sunjay Dutt and SRK to discuss the star. What each of these stars did was to reveal moments in their films when Madhuri had been encouraging and particularly helpful. The TV screen was arranged at split levels, with one section showing Madhuri listening with us to these comments and the other showing us the other star commenting on her. SRK confessed that he had learnt many histrionic skills when acting with Madhuri while Anil Kapoor and Sunjay Dutt revealed instances of Madhuri's commitment or rare talent.

Rakhi Sawant on *Koffee with Karan* (1 July 2007) admitted to cosmetic surgery, botox treatments and other interventions to acquire her body and face. She evaluated male stars from the industry on a scale of 1–10 for sex appeal (John Abraham got a '10' and SRK a '5'). She disclosed that she lived separately, that her father had abandoned them when she was 10, that her mother nagged her and that her parents did not like her. On other occasions Johar asks his guests about their fears, desires, families, questions that one would generally reserve for a more private conversation than one televised worldwide.

So what does a star who discloses hidden dreams and aspirations achieve? What the show emphasises is the social differential that makes *Koffee with Karan* significant. It is not a talk show where ordinary people appear. As opposed to talk shows where people, who otherwise have little media visibility appear, *Koffee with Karan* renders the celebrity more *immediate* through such personal queries and confessions, as does the less high-profile show *Idea Life Ban Jaye* on Sony. Although the show never lets us forget that we have a celebrity on screen, by detaching the celebrity from her or his usual appearance in a film, the show asks us to respond to them as people rather than stars or roles they play. By asking them to admit to personal tastes and dislikes, it gets the celebrity to shift slightly across the boundary that separates her or him from us. It makes the celebrity ordinary, one of us, *but all the while emphasising their uniqueness too*. We might call it a *hyper-mediated* setting, one that is carefully choreographed and made visible through the media, even as the media becomes self-effacing and invisible. Thus when Esha Deol admits on the show to spats with her mother, Hema Malini, we are given a glimpse of family life with the battle of the generations. *Koffee with Karan* is therefore a talk show that constantly *emphasises the celebrity-hood of the guest while seeking to unmask them*, maybe offer the audience a bit of their real self, with the whole programme embedded deeply within an ideology of intimacy.[17] It becomes yet another media ritual where they are simultaneously immediate and hyper-mediated.

Celebrity memoirs and shows are popular because, as in the case of Rakhi Sawant on *Koffee with Karan*, there is always a degree of authenticity associated with self-disclosure. As Jo Littler has argued, the ability to legitimise a '"moment before" fame' lends an air of authenticity (Littler 2003: 13). References to the time before they became famous (whether it is Jiah Khan about living in London and her real character[18] or Rakhi Sawant on her struggles to support the family) add the sense of reality and authenticity to figures that have become larger than life. The 'moment before fame' is what helps ordinary people, the audience, relate to the celebrity.

Media rituals also involve showing celebrities involved in everyday work and professions. Perhaps the best-known example in recent times is of A.P.J. Abdul Kalam, the former president of India. Often photographed interacting with school children and/or teaching, the celebrated scientist was known as the People's President. The act of teaching, when situating the President of India in the role of the teacher, was part of a media ritual where the great man or celebrity emphasised his ordinariness (since he left office in July 2007, he has accepted teaching positions in five universities in Tamil Nadu state). It grounded the president in ordinariness and demonstrated that he has not left behind or forgotten his roots. This media ritual also thrives on the ideology of intimacy. This is a central feature of celebrity culture. *The celebrity needs to constantly emphasise her or his ordinariness, adherence to family values or a work ethic while simultaneously fulfilling the audience's expectations and fantasies of glamour and lifestyle.* In fact, Phil Edgar-Jones, executive producer of the UK show, *Celebrity Big Brother*, declared, 'with normal Big Brother we're making ordinary people extraordinary. With this [Celebrity Big Brother], we're making famous people very, very ordinary' (Day 2007). *The process of ordinarisation or democratisation deconstructs traditional notions of celebrity, even as celebrity culture itself asks for a participatory democracy* with audience phone-ins and SMSs to select winners on *Indian Idol* or voting out participants from *Bigg Boss*.

Other talk shows that have found space on the Indian TV screen include the well known Oprah Winfrey and Phil Donohue. These are of a slightly different order of media ritual. Critics have argued that talk shows constitute an opportunity for ordinary people to have a public audience. It *makes them celebrities for being ordinary*, for possessing fears and anxieties, and for being able to talk about them (Grindstaff 1997). Television that normally excludes the ordinary, unless they are catastrophe survivors, becomes a means to achieve temporary stardom. It is an attempt to address social inequalities where only a few have access to public appearances and audiences. Something ordinary becomes something special where the fears of an ordinary person are taken seriously by the celebrity host.

Personal and intimate details become public knowledge through such confessions on camera. These should also be seen as forms of self-definition. You state what you are or what you think you are on camera, to a large, unseen audience and thereby commit yourself to an identity. New media facilitates, in different formats, similar acts of self-disclosure. Webcams, Blogs, personal webpages and groups like Orkut or Facebook are increasingly online versions of talk shows minus the host.

These also become sites of self-disclosure and awards like the Bloggies' award ensure a degree of celebrity status for the personal diary or memoir.

Media rituals that help construct a celebrity constitute *convergence*.[19] We know how much such and such a star commanded as a price for a particular film, how much a film cost and what collections it had in its opening week. Newspapers report huge advances paid to authors like Raj Kamal Jha and Vikram Seth and the exact amount Kiran Desai got as the Booker winner. The film celebrity, in particular, is mediated through a lot of *economic information* about the film itself.

Opening nights, film launches and previews are often attended by the stars themselves and reports of these circulate extensively in the news media. This is the public image circulation of the star in a *meta-filmic* context that is beyond the immediate context of the film and its narrative context—talking about the film, publicity about it and responses to the film.

Then there are the rituals of fan adulation, censorship, reviews, interviews, which are also part of the *meta-filmic* contexts along with news reports of celebrity scandals, lifestyles and their enormous wealth. Star images are always 'extensive, multimedia, intertextual' (Dyer 1986: 3). They are made of many texts, such as promos, biographies and gossip writing, in many media (such as movies and interviews). The star occupies an entirely different class and the media ritual of the shooting provides a space where we have access to or glimpses of the star.

In the case of sports stars, career record, product endorsements, bio- and autobiographical information, earnings and sponsorships all add up to the myth or image of the star. David Beckham's multi-million dollar deals shifting affiliations to clubs is an example, his latest deal with the US team LA Galaxy is reportedly worth UK£128 million. (BBC Sport Football 2007)

Celebrity product endorsements and political affiliations, alongside their specialised achievements, are all popularised by the media. The celebrities themselves, especially in recent times, have proudly declared their intentions of endorsing products for money. Thus SRK in 1998 said:

> I need money for my bungalow, I need money to secure my son's future. I need money to become financially firm. If that means plugging everything from colas to condoms, that's fine by me. (Chopra 2007: 158)

The aura of the celebrity is the result of all these individual and collective bits of information and themes coming together to us—a convergence. The economic, filmic, autobiographical, biographical details accumulate and create the effect of uniqueness. This is the celebrity.

A celebrity, in India particularly, has no domain restrictions. She or he is one who can cross any border, work across many domains. This could include meeting the prime minister of the country, commenting on a social crisis, contesting elections, promoting products and doing philanthropic work, even as she or he continues to make films or play cricket. The celebrity in India has this unique ability to move across fields of expertise. An expert in one area is deemed to be an expert in another. This is the symbolic and cultural capital made out of being a celebrity in any particular field. It is therefore possible to see the celebrity as *liminal*, as a person who belongs nowhere and everywhere, one who can move across borders into different sections of society.

Now, we have one more addition to the definition of celebrity. *A celebrity is the effect of a convergence of themes and kinds of mediated information, and is situated at a point from where she or he can move into any area other than her or his chosen field of expertise.* It is this simultaneous centripetal and centrifugal movement that marks a celebrity.

Celebrity and Consumer Culture

Products *named* or modelled, and commonly known by their film original, after movies or TV soaps, such as *Chandni* saris, *Kyonki Saas Bhi Kabhi Bahu Thi* bindis, *Maine Pyar Kiya* caps, *Lakshya's* jhola and crinkly skirts, *Fanaa's* skirts and kurtis, Farhan Akhthar's *Don's* paisley Shirts, *Dhoom 1's* Abhishek glasses, are celebrity consumer products. Nowhere is celebrity convergence more emphasised and prominent than in the consumer culture-celebrity culture linkage.

Central to the construction of a celebrity is her or his link with consumer and commodity culture, even as the celebrity integrates herself or himself into twentieth-century cultures of consumption.[20] Product endorsements and promotion constitute a key element in the public or social role of a celebrity.

Studies of consumer culture and advertising have demonstrated the influence of celebrity endorsement and signatures on consumers' attitudes to brands (Kamins et al. 1989; Frow 2002). This is partly attributed to the celebrity's credibility, recognition and public visibility.

Advertisements are forms of communication that come from various sources: the manufacturer, the marketing team, the public relations or publicity firm and the celebrity endorser. Our reaction to and acceptance of the information in an advertisement is informed by our perception of the credibility of these sources. For instance, why does a toothpaste advertisement require the Dental Association or Medical Association endorsement? Why do we respond differently to *Tata* Steel? The reason is that our perceptions of the medical body or the Tata company inform our perception of the product and the information in the advertisement. Would a product endorsed or advertised by a politician attract or possess credibility? (And that's a rhetorical question!)

Celebrity achievements become symbols of power, attractiveness and, finally, credibility. The Castrol engine oil advertisement is qualified by its perception of John Abraham's credibility. The stories of Abraham's rise to stardom (from an advertisement company executive, incidentally), the phenomenal success of the biker movie *Dhoom,* now better identified as *Dhoom I,* well-publicised information about his personal biking obsession, all contribute to the aura of credibility when he speaks in favour of Castrol. The advertisement relies on three aspects of this celebrity-*expert* (he is known to be an avid biker), *trustworthy* (since Abraham comes from a non-film background and has worked his way up, he has something in common with the non-privileged background Indian consumer) and *attractive* (John Abraham as iconic of the toned, fit and appealing body).

SRK advertises for Airtel's new scheme, the Super Star 501. An implicit connection is made between SRK's superstar status and reliability and the talk plan—'Airtel Presents Super Star 501 with Super Validity'.[21] A similar argument could be made about Aishwarya Rai or Sushmita Sen advertising for cosmetics. As winners of global beauty contests, they have extra credibility. Celebrity endorsements of products thus capitalise on the link between the perception of the celebrity's credibility and the product. Meaning is transferred from celebrity to product in three stages.

First, the meaning of the celebrity itself as attractive, reliable, influential, imitable. The celebrity becomes a role model, the MTV youth icon is an example, for particular sets of people. That is, symbolic meanings accrue to the celebrity. Thus Rahul Dravid 'The Wall' comes to represent reliability and efficiency. His work on the cricket field somehow becomes his chief characteristic and this meaning influences our perceptions of him in general. That is, the symbolic power of Dravid moves *beyond* the cricket field into other realms.

Second, the meaning transfers from the celebrity to the product. Dravid as the *reliable* cricketer endorsing life insurance or light bulbs transfers his chief value, that is, reliability, to the product.

Third, the consumer accepts and assimilates this meaning by buying the product endorsed by the celebrity. The consumer consumes the image of the celebrity via a consumption of the product she or he endorses—the reliability of a Dravid, the beauty of an Aishwarya Rai or the flair of a Dhoni. Dravid and Dhoni become, in Richard Dyer's adaptation of Lawrence

Alloway's work, 'maximised types' (Dyer 2002: 99). Dravid, Aishwarya Rai, Federer, Woods, Stephen Hawking embody the *maximum states of reliability, talent, looks and intellect possible*. Celebrity culture and product endorsements work on the basic principle that since Dravid is the epitome of reliability and Woods of efficient brilliance, the product or service they promote embody, symbolically at least, these qualities. Thus the products are also maximised. Hence Accenture's advertisement with Tiger Woods conflates his brilliance with its services—'High performance. Delivered'.

The point is that there is a close link between the perception of the celebrity and the product endorsed, where the product becomes a *transferred celebrity* as the qualities of the personality endorsing it merge with that of the product. Furthermore, the consumer seeks to associate herself or himself with the qualities of the celebrity through a consumption of their endorsed products. In this way, the celebrity is also assimilated and the status reinforced. A favourable response to a celebrity-endorsed product occurs only when consumers believe the qualities of the celebrity as worth emulating or desirable. Does one want to be like Aishwarya Rai? If so, buy the product she endorses.

The product mediates between the consumer and the celebrity of her or his choice in the form of the promotional rhetoric and eventual consumption. If a celebrity is a person whose achievements, lifestyle and behaviour serve as role models, then the consumer seeks to adopt those products and actions that the celebrity promotes as being most like him or her. Why else are (potential) consumers given details of Shilpa Shetty's home décor (*Hello!* July 2007) or information that Himesh Reshamiyya lives in a 'modest apartment overlooking the Versova beach',[22] and surveys of the houses of the rich and famous by magazines like *Society*? These are lifestyles we can aspire to, and they are role models for those who can afford Swarovski crystals and Persian rugs.

Tendulkar, the cultural icon of India's youth for his achievements in cricket, promotes energy drinks and food products.

Children who see him as somebody worth emulating seek to possess his prowess and talents. These are then transferred as qualities to the products he promotes. To drink this particular drink or to consume that particular brand of biscuits is to (*i*) show that we value Tendulkar's opinion since his performances prove that he knows best, (*ii*) demonstrate our willingness to emulate his feats—'ab to har ghar mein Sachin', as the advertisement goes. *Product endorsements thus extend and expand the celebrity's aura, just as consumer culture is central to the cult of the celebrity.*

Celebrity Bodies

In 1982, Amitabh Bachchan suffered an injury during the shooting of *Coolie*. There were nationwide prayers, cutting across language, religion and region for his safe recovery, a phenomenon never seen before in India. The film in its screening, even now, is frozen at the spot with a legend appearing on screen identifying it as the crucial moment of his injury, a reminder of the event that shook the nation. In February 2007, Saif Ali Khan suffered a mild cardiac arrest and made front page news. Reports and coverage of celebrity injuries or ailments are regular features of magazines and newspapers.

The coverage is symptomatic of the general interest in the celebrity *body*. The body of the celebrity is central to the culture, fan following and consumption of the celebrity. Chris Rojek referred to the aestheticisation of celebrities, whereby the 'perception and judgement regarding beauty and desire become generalized', a process we can discern in film and sports celebrities today (Rojek 2001: 102). Moreover, the aesthetically appealing celebrity is forgiven many other sins (as Cal Thomas, writing in the *International Herald Tribune* on Diana's 10th death anniversary, 2007, put it) because the masses only want to see good looks.

The carefully groomed look of Bollywood, including Priyanka Chopra, Kareena Kapoor, Katrina Kaif, Salman Khan, stars on

KBC and on *Koffee with Karan,* is part of their aura. Do we see celebrities minus their make-up, with acne, with excess fat or wrinkles? Occasionally we do and this lends the air of authenticity to the celebrity.

This is the paradox of celebrity bodies. We expect them to be perfect, that is, desirable but also, occasionally, we want to know that they are as human as the rest of us beneath the paint and beyond the flat abs. The body is what makes things happen for the celebrity or for anyone else. Hence the investment in the body is much higher for athletes, film stars and entertainer.

The perfect body of a celebrity represents the desirable body. It is no coincidence that gyms put up photographs of Salman Khan, Hrithik Roshan or John Abraham, the three stars whose toned physique often sets the benchmark for fit bodies. Gossip, tabloids and film magazines often inform us about overweight stars, cosmetic surgeries performed and ailments. The rush to see film shootings is actually a desire to see the star in the flesh *unmediated* (or so we like to believe) by cameras and special lighting. The enormous crowds at star shows are also the manifestation of this desire.

Celebrity bodies are often objects of often sexual desire. They represent perfect masculinity or femininity. They become models for what I term *body emulation* by youth. The frequent uproar over anorexic models is the expression of a concern that young girls wish to be waif-like because the women who win beauty pageants are waif-like and serve as fashion models.

Female stars, as critics have shown, seem to thrive on their bodies being desired or desirable. Perhaps the first such avowed projection of the sexually desirable icon of the twentieth-century screen was Marilyn Monroe (Dyer 1986: 42–50). The female star is the object longed for, the subject of fantasies and the perfect body that the man desires. The male body, especially in recent times (John Abraham, Salman Khan), becomes iconic of the ultra-masculine physique. In both cases, the celebrity body is one that is the subject of attention and attraction.

However, part of the appeal of the celebrity body is the roles essayed on screen, such as vamp, seductress-seducer, chaste heroine, macho hero and killer. SRK rarely plays an action hero, for instance, hence his body was rarely projected as an ultra-masculine one until *Om Shanti Om* (2007). He does not become the celebrity body for gyms and body-building regimens. On the other hand, Sunny Deol and Salman Khan and, more recently, John Abraham, have played the machismo role several times over. Their bodies therefore are both projected and consumed differently. There are, arguably, more pictures of Abraham and Salman Khan with their shirts off than there are of SRK, and SRK's sudden makeover with a six-pack body in *Om Shanti Om* is clearly a major shift in his celebrity look.

Hence, celebrity bodies also endorse products and appear on magazine covers. Once again, the particular image on the magazine cover or for the brand is drawn from the general image or role played by the celebrity, for example, the biker Abraham, the beautiful Aishwarya Rai.

What all this suggests is that *celebrity culture demands a body*. Or, to put it differently, celebrity is *embodied*. It is the body of the star that first contributes to the aura of the celebrity. Fame, therefore, resides at least partly in the face and the body of the celebrity.

A tangential version of this interest in celebrity bodies is the commodification of the star as a voyeur's delight or a sex object. Sneak photographs of Kareena and Shahid Kapur kissing did the rounds a couple of years ago. Magazines and tabloid gossip insinuate secret meetings, love nests and affairs between stars. Marital discord, sibling rivalry, sexual peccadilloes are all objects of curiosity and debate. These, once again, revolve around celebrity *bodies*—what they do, what they ought to do, who they do it with. Celebrity porn with morphed bodies and stalking and propositioning of celebrities are now integral to celebrity body culture.[23]

Increasingly, one suspects, there is a change in the representation of the celebrity body. From the perfect, chiselled and moral body, we now see a more sexualised, self-indulgent, even abused body. Bipasha Basu and Mallika Sherawat make no bones about their bodies. Celebrity talk now does not shy away from discussion of intimate details and relationships. Although naked celebrity bodies are not yet here, it appears that we are well on our way when we read about body modifications, their exercise regimen, their diets and their fashion preferences.

Cinema is surely one of the most powerful means for constructing the model body. The exercise scenes in Salman Khan films, the standard police beatings raining upon Sunny Deol's body and Abraham's lithe movements all suggest men who have resolved their anxieties about their bodies, and are at ease with the knowledge that they possess perfect bodies. The link between the body and the roles played—the beatings, the upright police officer, the infallible crook, the ultra-masculine man who can protect his girlfriend, wife mother sister or home—are ways of projecting the *lived* experience of such a body. That is, the film role often shows a character whose perfect, strong and masculine body helps him negotiate the stresses of life and society. Salman Khan, Sanjay Dutt and Sunny Deol use their bodies as a weapon in and of itself. The subtext suggests that such a body is an asset that helps resolve similar problems for others too. Or perhaps the celebrity body represents what Richard Dyer has called compensation, where stars 'compensate people for qualities lacking in their lives' (Dyer 2002: 28–30). This makes the celebrity male body desirable.

The perfect or perfectible body that Salman Khan or Bipasha Basu project is linked to the cult of the physical. Yoga, VLCC, diets, makeovers are now part of the lexicon in metropolitan India. In the age of newer diseases the body retains its centrality and the celebrity demonstrates what any human can aspire to, of course with a lot of sweat and toil and tasteless food! Health columns in magazines advise people on the right kind of food to eat. Physical trainers advise on the proper exercise regimen, even as some warn the youth that trying to acquire a celebrity body via a strict exercise and diet routine may not always be advisable (Pandey 2007). Local magazines such as *Bharatiya Kushti* and *Yog Manjari* also promote an Indian model of health and masculine fitness.[24] Other English language magazines like *Men's Health* and *Woman's Era*, likewise, offer suggestions on healthy living, exercise and makeovers. Oil manufacturers promote cholesterol-free and healthy oils. And VLCC advertises the slim, fit body. One must see the celebrity body as located at the end of this continuum even if they have not been through this same regimen.

Celebrity bodies serve to fix a particular form or beauty as a type or model (Dyer 2002: 14). That is, celebrity bodies define norms of attractiveness and beauty. The muscular male body (Salman Khan), the slender and toned woman (Bipasha Basu), the athletic body (Sania Mirza) generate a social meaning that *this* or *that* kind of look is 'in'.

All celebrity bodies are *staged* celebrities: self-projected fashionistas, socialites and stars with recognisability. The celebrity body is always on stage, always performing. Integral to the cult of the celebrity is therefore *the body that is always available to be viewed in its perfection*. This is the aestheticisation and staging of the celebrity body. The theatrical arrival of stars at a function or the photo shoot inside their homes (the Poonawalla family in the April 2007 issue and Shilpa Shetty at home in the July 2007 issue of *Hello!*—examples can be multiplied). The celebrity body is always on display, groomed, beautiful and desirable. It is rare that you come across dishevelled stars. If they are, then the dishevelment is also staged! It is therefore possible to conclude that celebrity bodies are on perpetual display. The fans, the audience *demand* it. In fact, it is the possibility of being on perpetual exhibition that marks a celebrity body.[25]

Another kind of celebrity body, far removed from the film or sport star, would be that of the author. Arundhati Roy campaigning for the people displaced by the Narmada, Salman Rushdie photographed with Padma Lakshmi in New York and Amartya Sen in newspaper photographs are examples of the 'mediagenic author' (a term I adapt from Joe Moran 2000: 35). Authorship is now not merely about the writing of a book, but also involves high profile book launches, reading tours, interviews to news papers and TV channels, extracts published in various places and reviews. Books are sold *through* the mass media and involve extensive photo coverage of the author. In the case of Roy, her public persona may have altered her status from celebrity author to a public intellectual, but rarely does one see a mention of her name without the tag 'Booker winner'. J.K. Rowling is of course the mediagenic author *par excellence* for the careful orchestration of her life and appearance—her early poverty, single mother-hood, stardom. Rowling is, arguably, even more famous than her literary creation. I suggest that every website, magazine essay, caricature, computer game and product remotely associated with Harry Potter, in fact, adds less to Potter than to Rowling. The fact is that she keeps an unprecedented control over productions of such material, and reinforces the aura of the author). P. Sainath's recent Magsasay Award has endorsed his public appeal as a journalist with a cause. In all these cases, the author has become a recognisable face in the mass media, at least in metropolitan contexts. Authorship here is carefully tied in to the machinery of cultural production that involves marketing, publicity and media coverage. The author is also now a brand packaged and sold through the media as best seller, socially concerned writer, rags-to-riches author or writer/activist. Literary celebrity is now increasingly the product of regular celebrity mechanisms of media, marketing and consumption. The ecology of the celebrity author is one that she or he shares with the film star and the politician.

Notes

1. *Movie*, July 2007, p. 10.
2. For example, a week before the *Indian Idol* finals, A.L. Chougule initiates a 'guessing game about 'Who Will Rule the Roost'. See, Chougule (2007).
3. I take the idea of the two economies of popular culture from Fiske (1987: 309–26).

4. On sports stars as role models see Lines (2001).
5. For a study of Tendulkar's role as celebrity and national icon, see, among others, Mazumdar (2004) and Nalapat and Parker (2005).
6. On media rituals, see, Couldry (2003).
7. 'Texas American Idol auditions draw over 12,000', 7 August 2007, http://www.actressarchives.com/news.php?id=7245; 'Thousands Line Up in San Diego for "American Idol" Season 7 Auditions', *Fox News*, 31 July 2007, http://www.foxnews.com/story/0,2933,291451,00.html; see also Stickney and Proskocil, '"Idol" Audition Crowd Thins Out in the Afternoon', *Omaha World Herald*, 9 August 2007, http://www.omaha.com/index.php?u_page=2620&u_sid=10103018
8. In 2008 we can add to the list Carla Bruni, the French President's girlfriend, whose nude photographs have appeared on blogs and magazines (http://lifestyle.indiatimes.com/Celebrity/Carla_Brunis_naked_snaps_published_/articleshow/2727111.cms [downloaded on 27 January 2008]).
9. *Candid Camera* involved using cameras in everyday life on people going about their business and literally setting them up in situations. This involved using props, dramatic situations and bizarre behaviour. For instance, Pogo's *Just for Laughs: Gags* has dummies on wheel chairs let loose across busy roads, even as the horrified expression of passers-by is recorded on camera.
10. Barbara Myerhoff, cited in O'Leary (1996: 795).
11. For a discussion on the physical setting of *Lagaan*, see, Raval (2001).
12. Of all the mediated memorial sites, perhaps the most astonishing are the electronic ones, for example the websites mourning Princess Diana. The unusual depth and multi-cultural mourning for Diana has been the subject of many essays and studies, most of which show how her celebrity status informed the cult of mourning. See, in particular, Kear and Steinberg (1999) and Helmers (2001).
13. http://www.setindia.com/biggboss/press.html, 17 September 2007
14. http://www.ibnlive.com/news/spotted-brangelina-in-mumbai/26034-8-single.html, 12 November 2006 (downloaded on 17 September 2007).
15. Oprah is perhaps the world's best known talk show host, a celebrity herself. The daytime talk show she has hosted for over 20 seasons now, reached its highest, most spectacular peak on 13 September 2004 when she handed over keys to brand new sports sedans from Pontiac to all 267 members of her studio audience as a surprise gift—an event unprecedented in television history.
16. On blogs as autobiography and diaries see, Rak (2005) and Sorapure (2005). A celebrity blog would be Professor Juan RI Cole's *Informed*

Comment (http://www.juancole.com/2004_04_01_juancole_
archive.html). Cole's comments on the Iraq war, published on this
blog, might have cost him his tenure at Yale. See, *Chronicle of Higher
Education* 52.47 (2006).

17. Here it differs from the film magazine (print) where similar questions are asked of the star but where the immediacy of the camera
is absent.

18. Interview, 28 February 2007. Available online at http://www.
movietalkies.com/interviews/view-interview.asp?InterviewId=143
(downloaded on 29 July 2007).

19. Graeme Turner sees convergence as the merging of systems of
delivery in the media, where entertainment and information industries are now one (33). Turner suggests that what marks the new
celebrity culture is the 'importance of the celebrity as a branding
mechanism for media products that has assisted their fluent transla-
tion across media formats and systems of delivery' (34). Thus TV
serials on cell phones, announced by Doordarshan, and its Digital
Terrestrial Telecast (DTT) technology thus far controlled only by
Doordarshan, will bring celebrities 24×7 even without a TV screen, a
kind of mobile celebrity culture (Bhattacharya 2007: 23). I use the
term convergence to indicate not so much the forms of media as the
themes—economic, consumer, fashion, specialised achievements,
social reponsibility—themselves. Thus the film star is not simply
about films, but about social responsibility (Priety Zinta's campaign
to keep Mumbai clean, or AIDS), political power (Amitabh Bachchan
and before him, M.G. Ramachandran and N.T. Rama Rao) and
consumer culture (Tendulkar's product endorsements).

20. On the cultures of consumption in the twentieth century see, among
others, Featherstone (1991).

21. *Deccan Chronicle*, 14 May 2007, p. 20.

22. *Society*, May 2007, p. 44.

23. On celebrity porn see, Turner (2004: 122–7). On fans stalking
celebrities see, Cashmore (2006: 90–4).

24. For a reading of these magazines and the cult of the physically fit,
male body in post-Independence India see, Alter (2004). For a
similar study of the idea of physical development in Western culture
see, Dutton (1995).

25. Celetoids or criminals do not, however, require this kind of perpetual
staging. But then criminal bodies are not to be seen as imitable either.
Victims bodies such as the prisoners in Abu Ghraib or Gauntanamo
Bay, Holocaust visuals of emaciated Jews in Auschwitz and other
camps, and even celetoids like Mohammed Haneef (arrested and
incarcerated in Australia in 2007 under suspicion of being a terrorist) are celebrity bodies by virtue of being ruined or traumatised.

3

Star Power: The Celebrity as Spectacle

*We have many wonderful events taking place across London through-
out the three month duration of India Now and the world premiere of
Chak De India will undoubtedly be one of the biggest and most exciting. It is a great honour for London to host this launch event for a film,
which, like so many Bollywood blockbusters, will touch the hearts and
minds of millions across the world.*

— Ken Livingstone, Mayor of London, on the premiere
of *Chak De India* at Somerset House, London[1]

One way of understanding the production of a celebrity is
to classify her or him as a spectacle that focuses an
individual or collective abstract desire, a process that
Chris Rojek terms 'celebrification' (Rojek 2001: 186–7). Celebrities embody abstract desire to achieve, to be recognised, to
be wealthy (poverty-stricken celebrities would be hard to find).
Celebrities represent what people aspire to be or to possess.
This process of celebrification is almost entirely media generated. Elements and styles of stars are refined and structured
by the mass media in ways that project particular identities
as desirable. In India, celebrities circulate in two ways—as a
perpetual *spectacle* and as an *extended* celebrification. Celebrification and its spectacle is perhaps the core process, the DNA,
of celebrity ecology.

Twentieth-century inaugurated the era of the 'media spectacle' (I adapt the term from Douglas Kellner [2003]). Politics,
economy, social problems, everyday life all takes the form
of spectacles. Murders, corruption cases, fashion, political

conflict, war, disease and death, sex scandals, the neighbour-hood hero are all enacted, available and visible as extravaganzas on *screen*, which here includes billboards, banners, posters, TV, film and print. Information and entertainment merge in infotainment, where entertainment is the key focus of television coverage and newspaper reportage. Spectacle implies, of course, something to be seen and an audience to do the seeing. That is, spectacle involves the *production* of something on screen and its consumption by the audience. Spectacle often dissociates us from everyday life because the screen and the events unfolding upon it enchant us. Here we are concerned with the production of celebrity spectacle, and shall return to the question of consuming celebrities later in the book.

A celebrity body, as noted earlier, is always *on*. What constitutes SRK or Sania Mirza as a celebrity is not only their skills in their respective professions but the 24×7 *visibility* of these skills for the consumer. The magazine *Filmfare*, for example, often carries letters in which readers complain there is far too much of SRK. This is an index of SRK's hyper-visibility. Celebrity culture would not be possible without media, and what the media does is to *transform particular bodies, faces, mannerisms, roles and events into viewable spectacles*. We consume the spectacle of the celebrity on screen. As a corollary, it could be argued that whatever attains adequate time through repetition (on screens, that is), it becomes a sustained spectacle, also becomes a celebrity. Spectacle is what makes certain people desirable, objects of fantasy and emulation. In short, spectacle is what renders the celebrity a celebrity, and all celebrities *perform* within the space of the spectacle.

Spectacle is linked to the media's shift in focus, perceivable from the late 1990s in India, from information and reportage to what Graeme Turner terms 'tabloidization' (Turner 1999). Newspapers today arguably give as much information about celebrities and celebrity events as other news. That is, what we have is more entertainment than news where soap opera replaces politics and celebrity talks replace social concerns. Unless, of course, celebrities are involved in the latter too.

Visibility is linked to the *contexts* in which stars operate. Contexts, as Ellis Cashmore (2006) constantly reminds us, are all-important in celebrity culture. Advertisements featuring SRK and Sania Mirza, for instance, build on prior knowledge of their skills and prior recognition of their talent and their respective contexts. The advertisement for Sunfeast biscuits, therefore, shows SRK performing a dance sequence and a comic turn. The Sprite advertisement shows Sania finishing a round of tennis. Both contextualise the product in terms of the celebrity's field of specialisation.

Within more specialised news reportage, Lalu Yadav becomes a celebrity politician as the minister who managed to miraculously transform Indian Railways into a profit-making organisation. In 2001 Indian Railways had defaulted payments to the tune of more than Rs. 18,230 million. By 2006 it was raking in profits, with a Rs. 121,400 million turnover. The celebrity status here, visible in the public domain by his Harvard talks and the IIM recognition of the miracle, is rendered all the more spectacular because of two incidental factors—the country's Prime Minister Manmohan Singh is a noted economist with Oxford-Cambridge academic credentials and the Finance Minister P. Chidambaram is a Harvard MBA. It is in this context of academically famous ministers that 16 students of the Post-graduate Programme in Management for Executives (PGPX), IIM-A debated *Lalu Yadav's* success story on 18 September 2006.

In sharp contrast to these two high-profile ministers, Lalu Yadav with his rural background becomes all the more spectacular for his achievements; even assuming that he was able to rely on a very efficient ministry and bureaucracy to do so. This is where the spectacle truly makes its presence felt. Lalu Yadav did not represent the success story as an economic miracle. Instead, he turned notions of spectacle on its head by retrieving rural metaphors to describe it. He declared that railway wagons are like 'a cow ready to be milked'. He then went on to add, 'You have to milk the cow, otherwise she will become sick. The railway wagons are giving profit but that's not enough, you have to maximize the use of wagons' (Bhatt 2006). Although this sounds suspiciously like a joke, it was not. Lalu Yadav was appropriating India's agrarian image to describe economic development and thereby making a spectacle. In the face of talk about information superhighway and globalised economy, Lalu turns the metaphor back to rural India and an act that most metropolitan Indians might have never seen—the milking of a cow. This is spectacle because it appears to mock urban elitism, economic theory and high-profile management institutions and doctrines. This aspect of spectacle of the newest celebrity politician is emphasised in a news item on the popular rediff.com. Sheela Bhatt writing about Lalu Yadav's IIM-A tryst wrote:

> Lalu Prasad Yadav wants to do something that even Amitabh Bachchan cannot do: an image makeover... The master tactician of Indian politics is embarking on a difficult assignment, of changing his brand-image... His PR advisors want the media to acknowledge him as Lalu Yadav, Master of Business Administration... The new venture, starring Lalu Yadav, has been scripted by himself and produced by his political ambition. (Bhatt 2006)

Note the film and theatre language of this news item: 'image makeover', 'brand image', 'starring', 'scripted' and 'produced'. The comparison with Amitabh Bachchan is also appropriate, for the kind of things it is saying. We are now talking of a Lalu Yadav economic theory and an organisational achievement that is conscious of the brand management possibilities. He is now a brand validated by the ultimate audience in its specialised field, the IIMs. The role of the media in projecting this new spectacle of a rural politician notorious for an administrative mess in Bihar (as the same article notes) is very clear. Lalu is the new brand, the new icon and the new spectacle who is different because he chooses his context-bound metaphors with care. This is the process of celebrification where the desire for efficiency, productivity and profit, features one does *not* associate with the public sector in India, is made visible as a concrete identity of the Indian Railways.

Celebrity spectacle also involves other specific features, of which aesthetic appeal is perhaps the most crucial. Admittedly, cricketing uniforms do not quite have the same level of appeal as a Manish Malhotra costume, but it is part of the process of *aestheticisation* where the star is dressed in clothes connected to her or his profession.

Aestheticisation, Fashion and Taste

I am not a very fashionable person ...I have my own style fundas. Anu Kaushik did my make-up but I did my hair myself. Otherwise, I am a very white-shirt-and-blue jeans kinda person.

— Puja Gupta, winner, Femina Miss India 2007[2]

Stars are everywhere.

1. Film magazines carry photographs.
2. Products, from biscuits to toys, have photographs of stars.
3. Websites have entire collections of photographs.
4. Posters of stars use photographs and artistic renderings.
5. Newspapers carry reports accompanied with visuals of star functions, film shoots and award ceremonies.
6. Cabs and other forms of public transport carry posters and photographs.

Photographs of film stars stare at you from hoardings, inside autorickshaws, fliers and notices and promotional material; they appear in newspapers and on television. The amount of visual material of a star renders the star more immediate, available and knowable. Famous people in the pre-photograph years were removed from the everyday lives of the common man. Kings and queens were celebrities, but one did not actually see them or their representations on a regular basis.

But, more to the point is that the star's face is something we always notice, stare at. The star is always *visible* and therefore has to always be appealing, even when caught in the most mundane of contexts. This is the aestheticisation of the celebrity in order for the person to appeal as a spectacle.

Aestheticisation is linked to the very public face of a celebrity. Even when a beauty contest winner such as Puja Gupta denies her fashionableness, as in the epigraph to this section, it firmly entrenches her in the visual field of looks, appeal, desirability and fashion. Aestheticisation is connected to the technologies of *recording* this public face and focussing the visual field on to or around the celebrity. Aesthetic appeal is primarily to the eye and this is the key to the spectacle of celebrity. Central to celebrity spectacle and its aestheticisation is the photograph.

Aestheticisation involves questions of taste, beauty and fashion. A celebrity must fit in with the new idiom of taste even as she or he sets the trend in taste. This is the paradox of celebrity culture. On the one hand, their aesthetic must be truly chic and appealing or else they could figure in lists of celebrities with wardrobe malfunction. On the other hand, they must break the fashion mould and start new trends for people to look up to and emulate, always a risky proposition.

Stars today have to be, therefore, hot, sexy, cool and happening. *Elle* Magazine uses as its ad line 'Sexy, Stylish, Spirited'. Celebrity is about *style*, in a culture increasingly subject to the anxiety of appearance. New definitions and ideas of what is hot occur in the media. Thus MSN, in April 2007, conducted a poll to find 'the new definition of sexy'. Jeremy Egner's write-up on the poll described contemporary American culture as apparently valuing 'air-brushed visual titillation' (Egner 2007).

Fashion is a key element in consumer culture. The fashion show, with the sashaying models, the laser lighting, the music, the audience, all with a high glamour quotient, is clearly a spectacle where taste, consumption and profits merge. These bodies—many of which move into films—and contests, such as Graviera India, provide the launch pad for fashion celebrities.

Likewise, music-video television (MTV) and the widespread contest culture for singers and musicians use music as a means of *both* fashion spectacle and celebrity culture.

The descriptions of celebrity clothes, including wardrobe disasters, in film magazines are also about constructing the star body as the benchmark in perfectibility. The reference to brands—'so and so wore a Manish Malhotra dress', Rakhi Sawant on *Koffee with Karan,* declared with some pride that she was wearing a Manish Malhotra dress, is an invitation to emulate, a mode of suggesting where to shop for whatever the celebrity wore. In short, it draws a link between the celebrity's body and that of the individual reader's *via* consumer culture—'even you can *buy* and *wear* what X wore'. Celebrity fashions and bodies are therefore, especially in the case of writing about women's fashions, about *consumer culture that emphasises the cult of the perfectible body.* Furthermore, by showcasing the star's body and clothes, the writing emphasises the taste, choice and ability of the star. She chooses what to wear and how to look, and you can do the same. Aishwarya Rai arriving at the Cannes film festival (2007) may be the most beautiful woman in the world, but not all her celebrity appeal or beauty is natural. Her clothes, accessories, body language are all carefully cultivated and groomed. Critics have suggested that magazines like *heat*, and fashion writing in magazines, show the empowerment of women, perhaps best captured in L'Oreal's slogan—'because you are worth it'. There is no reference to looking good *for anyone*, it is entirely for her own self that the woman focusses on her looks, career, pleasure and body. Feminine fashion and consumer culture can be treated as part of a feminist stance where individual choice is supreme.[3] The celebrity, used as a role model, embodies this empowered woman—part natural, part artifice.

The beautified celebrity body provides an intriguing relationship between surface appearance and social class. As Joanna Entwhistle has argued about fashion and identity, it is possible to see designer clothes-fashion industry-celebrity body as constituting a plane of consumption (Entwhistle 2000). The celebrity body acquires an identity partly through fashion. It separates the celebrity body from the other bodies. Second, the same fashions can be acquired because the designers open retail outlets for anyone who can afford it. Fashion becomes a source of personal or self-development for the individual. In a sense, celebrity fashions offer the *potential* to participate in or belong to that same class. Thus when individual designers start their own lines and retail outlets, for example, John Abraham in India or Angelina Jolie in the USA, they are *expanding their celebrity culture outwards*. Fashion becomes a marker not only of a person's individual identity but, through the shared fashion system and designer labels, of her or his affiliations and social circle. Celebrity bodies thus become models for social differentiation—those who can afford to get versions of celebrity fashions from the same designer and those who cannot—even when the celebrity model is not a member of that social circle.[4]

Fashion is a mode of body culture in order to attain social solidarity and recognition. Fashion redefines the body as spectacle in the case of the celebrity. According to at least one website, fashion designer Manish Malhotra believes SRK is the best-dressed star.[5] But why is it important to know this? Celebrities are icons of consumption because their fashion or taste become models of consumption for others to follow (Dyer 2002: 39–40). Their lifestyle, clothing, accessories, houses, leisure provide a role model for society, setting up a chain of consumption. Celebrities use fashion to both advance and alter their personality in the public gaze. They constitute themselves as people with particular tastes, and therefore representing not only a particular class but also as a body worth emulating. This aligns aestheticisation with not only body culture but also with *social appeal*.

What the star or celebrity wears is crucial to her or his appeal. Thus the fact that SRK wore a Manish Malhotra creation or Gauri Khan was seen in a Shane and Falguni Peacock ensemble is as much about SRK-Gauri Khan as it is about Malhotra and the Peacocks. Malhotra and the Peacocks are arguably *as famous as the celebrities they dress*. When the Peacocks' website lists and showcases the celebrities they have dressed, they each thrive off each other as independent, symbiotically connected celebrities.[6] This is a whole new semiotics of celebrity culture where the celebrity's fashion designer is a celebrity her or himself. What was once an accessory that derived its appeal from association with the celebrity body is now an independent celebrity.

Social appeal and desirability are arguably the most significant effects of celebrity fashion. The amount of attention paid to what's in or what's cool suggests an increasing emphasis on the aesthetic appeal of the public face or body and celebrities, located where they are (in the camera's eye).

What is important is to be seen as cool or sexy. Celebrity aestheticisation is linked to a social process of beautification. It suggests social solidarity and group membership by setting an *agenda* for aestheticisation. The aestheticisation of celebrity bodies occurs through several modes.

To begin with, there is the enormous amount of description of what so-and-so was wearing. To take a recent example, the coverage of a celebrity wedding, that of Arun Nayar and Elizabeth Hurley, as covered by *Hello!* magazine in its inaugural Indian issue (April 2007). The article was titled 'Elizabeth Hurley and Arun Nayar Wed in Style at Sudeley Castle, and Later in Jodhpur'. 'It was always going to be a spectacular affair' is the opening line. The first paragraph ends with 'Damian, who held on proudly onto the veil of his mother's hand-made chiffon Versace wedding gown'. Later she changed into a Versace Atelier 'goddess' evening gown. We are told that Hurley had:

> Dazzled throughout the week in a succession of stunning outfits, including a Dolce and Gabbana cocktail dress, a Dior Coutore gown teamed with Chopard jewellery, a silver and white *sangeet* dancing dress by top Indian designer Rohit Bal, couture evening dresses by Roberto Cavalli and Jenny Peckham, and a ravishing Versace Couture wedding dress. (*Hello!* April 2007)

The groom, we are informed, had 'three pairs of couture shoes' made for him by Patrick Cox and Indian costumes made by Rohit Bal. The guests were 'wearing saris, suits and jewels from boutiques personally recommended by Elizabeth and Arun'. Elizabeth later wore 'a hot pink silk sari by Tarun Tahiliani'. While awaiting her guests she wore a red Valentino dress.

If the Hurley-Nayar wedding took up massive photo and report space, it was immediately followed by the Abhishek-Aishwarya Rai wedding. *Filmfare* went so far as to declare that the Hurley-Nayar one may 'have got their share of media space', but 'nothing compares to this one'.[7] Although photo coverage of the wedding was minimal in *Filmfare*, we are duly informed that 'Ash stuck to her favourite designer Neeta Lulla' and 'Abhishek's wedding trousseau was designed by Kolkata-based designer Sharbari Datta'.[8]

The event is rendered more spectacular for the ways in which the bodies of the participants are transformed into displays. Aestheticisation is this process of staging the celebrity body as a fashion statement.

Filmfare's report on the 52nd Annual Fair One Filmfare Awards, 2007 began by telling us how it was to be exclusive. Its promos on TV had Karan Johar and Amitabh telling us how it was to be very elite and exclusive.

> Sprawling maidans made way to an indoor venue which would hold an audience of just about 700. Assembly line item numbers were replaced by carefully selected, perfectly choreographed, pre-recorded performances. Hordes of screaming audience would go missing and, instead, we would have an intimate evening designed just for the *crème de la crème*.

This 'black tie' event with 'admission restricted', wrote Sukanya Venkatraghavan, 'would restore Filmfare Awards its dignity and class'.[9] The grounds are laid. It is an exclusive function for the very elite. As we have noted, the *context* of the celebrity is crucial. If the Hurley-Nayar wedding was declared 'an event

of national importance' by locals—apparently photographs of
the couple were displayed in shop windows in Jodhpur even
before the wedding, according to *Hello!*—the Filmfare Awards
were described as a 'paradigm shift in the format of award
functions'.[10]

In this black tie celebrity event, fashion takes up the greatest
media coverage. Sameera Reddy was in an orange sari; Rekha
was 'resplendent in a red *kanjeevaram* sari with a hip short
border'; Kelly Dorje wore a tux and a bow tie, said the fashion
catalogue; then, as if to emphasise the point, the magazine had
an entire section called 'Filmfare Fashion 2007'.

> Our gals looked and felt like a million dollars ... new standards have
> been set and life, or for that matter fashion, will never be the same
> any more.[11]

This write-up introduces the fashions on display at the event.
Visuals of women are placed in long, narrow boxes lending an
additional slimness to the figure, and a short legend describing
the dress and its designer. There was a section for male stars
too. Interestingly, there were more full-length photographs of
the women than the men. Stars were also asked to identify their
favourite and best-dressed fellow stars. Such peer evaluation
of each other's fashion and taste returns us to the argument
of social solidarity. Rohit Bal, Malaika Arora Khan and Cyrus
Broacha appeared on *Koffee with Karan* to adjudicate the best
dressed celebrity on the show.

Significantly, the next issue of the magazine had a section
devoted to 'fashionmiss.ya.misses' where they photographed
stars in what the magazine called 'anti-fashion'.[12] To be a
celebrity is to apparently be always well dressed and hip.
Such attention to fashion and taste is not always restricted
to celebrity *events*. Anna Kournikova, perhaps better known
for her looks than her tennis, is photographed more in normal
clothing than in sports gear. Tendulkar, on the other hand,
is more often photographed or filmed in sports gear. After
Dhoom II, Hrithik's Honda bike advertisement shows him in
racing gear. John Abraham's first bike advertisements, with

the hero in racing gear, ran after *Dhoom 1*, once again linking the fiction-film with the fiction-advertisement through fashion even though the focus is supposedly the bike.

The process of the celebrity dressing up, however, is not the only dimension to such an aestheticisation. A lot depends on who *else* is dressing up. In the Hurley-Nayar wedding, for instance, we also find details about the other guests. Elton John, Parameshwar and Adi Godrej, assorted princes and billionaires (the descriptive occurs several times in the report). There is an implicit assumption that readers would recognise the designers and their specialisations. This presupposes, therefore that there exists a certain kind of clientele that would read the article and be familiar with designer clothes and jewellery. There is also the related phenomenon that designers like Rohit Bal also model for clothes—Line Club Fabrics, an Aditya Birla Group line.

Aestheticisation is thus a marker of social solidarity here. *Everybody who comes to the wedding would be equally fashionable and wealthy* and this is precisely what the report highlights. Fashion and social relationships seem to reflect and complement each other. It is indeed a community of the fashionable, a social fabric, if you please.

We have opinion polls on star wear on the best dressed and the worst dressed. Thus even websites catering apparently to Indians abroad want to keep their readers informed about celebrity clothes and fashions. Describing the F Awards—For Excellence in Indian Fashion award ceremony at the Taj Land's End (Mumbai), one report, dated 13 November 2004, rated Aishwarya Rai as the best and Shoaib Akhtar as the worst dressed people.[13]

Then we have celebrity product endorsements. John Abraham's carefully cultivated ultra-machismo looks and Sachin Tendulkar's energetic batting both get aestheticised. Abraham's Yamaha advertisement emphasises the macho image of biking. Tendulkar's demanding field requires higher energy and therefore the Boost advertisement projects him as an active man. The aesthetic here is in the kind of roles shown to us. Abraham, after the phenomenal success of *Dhoom 1*, fitted into the aesthetics of machismo biking. Tendulkar, arguably India's most successful cricketer, likewise fits into the aesthetics of health and energy suggested by the drink. This linkage of aesthetics with both celebrity contexts and consumerism is celebrity culture.

Taken together these represent a large amount of texts that constitute celebrity fashion, but with a difference. The spectacle here does not only represent something unique out there, it also represents a fashion or product that can be acquired. Celebrity aestheticisation renders us even more aspirational consumers (Cashmore 2006: 58) where we buy not to subsist but to show our progress in the world. Celebrity aesthetics is linked with consumerism via a media blitz of product endorsements. We desire or acquire a product so that we are closer to the person projected in the advertisement. This is precisely how advertisements work. As David Lewis and Darren Bridger put it:

> New consumers are really seeking to discover themselves. Not the people they feel themselves to be at this moment, but the kind of men and women they aspire to be and feel it is within their power to become. (Cashmore 2006: 175)

Unlike sports stars whose celebrity status is linked very often with their achievements in the field, though it is not unconnected to fashion, others often need to underscore a stunning appearance as a marker of their celebrity-hood.

This emphasis on looks and taste in celebrity dressing also filters down as a consumer commodity. This is *extended celebrification*, where celebrity tastes and preferences become starting points for not only product endorsements but also to evaluate standards of taste in *other* areas of life.

To begin with, celebrities set up standards of taste and fashion. Secondly, looks and fashion attain the aura of acquirable objects, given enough expenditure of time, money and energy. Thirdly, Bollywood stars are often called in to judge or be spectators at fashion shows, walk the ramp for their favourite designers, store inaugurations and television contests, thus making the link between celebrity-hood, fashion and spectacle even more obvious. Finally, celebrity culture directly moves into consumerism when stars launch their own signature lines of clothing or accessories.

The discourse of fashion or style unites celebrities from different backgrounds (such as Yuvraj Singh and Yash Birla, Sachin Tendulkar and SRK, Sania Mirza and Parmeshwar Godrej). Celebrity fashion rhetoric does not treat them as representative of their specific fields but rather as common fashion icons. This condition of spectacle that breaks down career distinctions converts all celebrities into entertainment images and commodities. Their recognition is based less on their successes in particular fields than as trendsetters, faces at mega events and fashion icons. Do we know exactly what Yash Birla does or Adar Poonawalla has achieved? An individual celebrated for achievements in one domain is appreciated in another, entirely different one. Singers, socialites, sport stars, film actors or actresses, business tycoons are all the same and *interchangeable*, grist to the fashion mill in a democratisation of fashion. Celebrity culture homogenizes achievements under the rubric of 'style'.[14]

Since celebrities are, or become, indices of fashion, it is automatically assumed that to wear or use their products is fashionable. Fibre2Fashion, a fashion and textile portal, reported in February 2007 that numerous Indian film stars were now emulating Hollywood icons and launching their own lines. In Hollywood, Jennifer Lopez, Elizabeth Hurley, Eminem, Will Smith, Spike Lee, Britney Spears have launched their own lines in fashion clothing and accessories. The stars who are working on their own lines include Fardeen Khan, John Abraham, Malaika Arora Khan and Hrithik Roshan. How exactly does a celebrity design a line since his or her expertise in the area is often limited to listening to advice and wearing the appropriate clothing?

John Abraham's line of clothing from Wrangler will have 'small notes sticking out from the inside pockets containing his comments on the design, style and how he came up with the look'. ITC's John Player, now endorsed by Hrithik Roshan, will soon provide a signature line that will try to 'bring alive the brand and establish a style statement for the star (Hrithik) for a specific character'. Malaika Arora Khan wants to bring out her own line which would be 'an extension of her identity'.[15] 'Tiger Eyes by SRK' range of perfumes from the French perfume specialist Jeanne Arthes was announced in 2005. Amitabh Bachchan has Blue, a perfume for women, created by Lomani. The emphasis on the star's personality as stamped on the product they create shifts celebrity content from its designated areas elsewhere as extended celebrification.

Celebrities move out of their fictional constructions—film— or fields of specialisation, for example, sport, into real life when they advice people on clothing, food and life. The US magazine *heat*, 4–10 December 2004, carried advice from Sarah Jessica Parker, established as a celebrity after her *Sex and the City*, on accessories, while the magazine offered advice on more affordable versions of SJP's style. They offer tips on fitness, grooming, style and love, some of them inane. Pamela Anderson, for example, offered her personal tip on fitness, reported by Asia Features in *Deccan Chronicle*—stay fit by avoiding snacking.[16] Others provide insights and information into their own personal tastes and habits that are located somewhere between inspirational rhetoric and self-publicity.

Their own bodies and lives become the goal of the consumer or reader. The star's home, family, exercise regimen and diet become possible role models for them. For instance, the happy family-happy home portrait of Sridevi-Boney Kapoor and their daughters in the May 2007 issue of *Filmfare*, or the constant news reportage of Britney Spears' child custody problems and mothering habits.[17] Although the wealth may not be as easily secured, the looks, especially with cheaper imitations, and fitness certainly can. John Abraham, Hrithik Roshan and Salman Khan thus become models for the fit macho body and adorn the walls of gyms. Magazines like *Men's Health* continually render the muscled, hyper-masculine male body as a spectacle, while also making the body an icon of fashion and consumption (Nayar 2008). The sporting bodies of David Beckham, Roger Federer, Sachin Tendulkar 'emblematise' hard work outs, fitness and high levels of achievement often purchased at the cost of pain and suffering. All sports stars have a history of injuries that are well-publicised.[18] A range of cosmetic products, exercise regimen, clothing and accessories constitutes the rhetoric of celebrity masculinity using fashion models. These in turn become the emulatable male body, or what Susan Alexander has called *branded masculinity* (Alexander 2003). There is therefore a clear link between the iconic bodies of Salman Khan or John Abraham, their role as fashion models and brand ambassadors, and consumer society, a link that thrives, indeed subsists on the culture of fashion spectacle. They generate what is now called *fitness chic* (Whannel 2002: 70–4, 131–2).

The celebrity magazine provides its readers with 'a fashionable window in which star styles are on display' (Feasey 2006: 183–4). Attention is also paid, to the embarrassment and anger of the celebrities, to what is termed wardrobe malfunction. Reporting the Lakme Fashion Week in March 2006, the anonymous author mentioned several malfunctions, from 'slipping bustiers' to 'busted zippers', and how 'many in the crowd caught the embarrassing moments using cameras in their mobile phones'.[19] The magazine thus functions as an arbiter of taste and fashion in its comments on the best dressed and worst dressed celebrities. *Deccan Chronicle*, Hyderabad city's largest circulating newspaper, carries a weekly recipe from one film star, thereby expanding the cult of celebrity expertise and celebrity taste. *Filmfare* carries, as part of the promotional material for Daawat *basmati* rice, a column titled 'Taste Buds Speak' where stars speak of their food preferences. We are even informed of new trends in celebrity food habits, when for instance, the *Deccan Chronicle*, carried a news item on the celebrities who had turned vegetarian because they were dating people who were vegan. A new term to describe these types is 'vegan sexual' (Toshniwal 2007: 21).

The Ordinary as Celebrity

Celebrity spectacle and coverage spills over into the spectacle of the everyday too. Celebrity culture suggests the possibility of acquiring a special face or a unique personality that sets one on the road to fortune or stardom. This cult of celebrity fashion, disseminated by more and more amounts of information about celebrity life, has resulted in the proliferation of grooming schools, fashion advice columns and everyday tips for good dressing and grooming.

Filmfare carries a regular column where they pick an ordinary woman or man and undertake a makeover, and this column is often titled symbolically. In 'The Making of a Cinderella' (May 2007), the candidate is transformed from a 'reticent Ritika' into 'a super confident girl with a body language that oozed confidence'. *Hello!* in its inaugural Indian issue advised women on make-up, using Nicole Kidman, Julia Roberts, Christina Aguilera, Jessica Simpson and Jennifer Lopez as examples for particular kinds of looks, and terming the various products 'must-have cult beauty products'.[20] Amstech Finishing School in Hyderabad advertises itself locally in the newspapers with a tagline 'Complete Women are Made in Finishing Schools'. *Verve* magazine carries a 'Trend Forecast' column so that one can stay informed about what is hip or cool. The Fair and Lovely advertisement shows how an ordinary looking girl with the usual skin problems of her age first lands a commentator's job and is then noticed by K. Srikkant in the commentary box because she is transformed.

Ordinary people see celebrities from a distance, on television, on the screen or in a crowd. However, it is increasingly possible to meet celebrities in restaurants, public spaces and stores. This results in an interesting intersection between the ordinary and the extraordinary in the audience's frame. It results in an interesting paradox. We have seen and known the celebrity for some time now via celebrification and media.

In this sense, the celebrity is intimate. However, we are now encountering the celebrity in the flesh for the first time. This meeting is therefore situated at a problematic junction of the intimate and the stranger and constitutes a special spectacle.[21]

The spectacle of celebrity, however, is not restricted to such a sighting. On the contrary, I suggest that the extraordinary proliferation of celebrity information, lifestyles and personal details has resulted in a culture of *possible emulation* that constitutes a second-order spectacle. By second-order I do not mean secondary, but rather the *spectacle generated through fashions, standards of taste and designer clothing that invites an ordinary person to try on the look of the celebrity.* Second-order spectacle is integrally linked to celebrity culture because fashion is driven by celebrities, whether modelling for the line, endorsing it or wearing it on screen. On the one hand, this second-order spectacle asks you to do your own thing (the magazine dedicated to younger women, *GURLZ* uses as its advertisement line 'Express your own style'). On the other hand, it uses celebrities to propose possible *models* for you to do your own thing. In many women's magazines there is a touch of the feminist which suggests that they dress up to feel good for themselves. L'Oreal's famous 'Because I am Worth It' shifted emphasis from looking good for others to doing things for one's own pleasure.

In a sense this is part of the spectacle industry where, by watching and emulating a celebrity spectacle, one might aspire to the looks and identity of the star. Second-order spectacle is more often than not high fashion, though low-budget fashions are also increasingly visible.

Second-order spectacle is a component of the para-social relationship with the celebrity. Para-social relationships are *imagined* connections to celebrities, a kind of surrogate for actual friendships or other relations. Second-order spectacle locates one in particular relation to the celebrity, as imitating, aspiring to be like X or as fashionable as a star. It is often as fashion consumerism that such a second-order spectacle emerges. If celebrity spectacle is mostly singular, it generates a second-order spectacle that is *collective* when more people adopt a fashion.

Second-order spectacle is not simply derivative because consumers *adapt* fashion, indigenise and localise it on a regular basis. Second order spectacle can be treated as a separate order of fashion that emulates celebrity with a difference. As examples of such a second-order spectacle, one can think of the fashion accessories that hit the market after particular films. The cool neck tag of SRK in *Kuch Kuch Hota Hai*, the Preity Zinta glasses after *Kal Ho Naa Ho* and the thick frame glasses after Abhishek Bachchan in *Dhoom 1*.

There is, however, a different kind of celebrity possible now. Ordinary people, the girl next door or the unimpressive classmate can become a celebrity in the space of a few months. This demotic turn in celebrity culture allows the ordinary people, with the help of the media, the widespread contest culture and makeover options to become celebrities.[22] This demotic turn is partly the result of globalised media. With more and more channels, television companies battle each other for better advertisements and higher TRPs. For this, they reinvented both television's content and form. As the number of movies that could possibly be bought and telecast on the many channels began to get smaller, television invented the *contest* and the *game show. Indian Idol*, in its third season in 2007, launched in 2004 and described by Albert Almeida, the Executive Vice President and Business head of Sony Entertainment Television, as 'the ultimate platform for any budding singing talent' (Almeida 2007: 72) is only one in a long line of similar television contests devoted to various talents like singing, dancing, acting and quizzing.[23] 'Superstar', 'Antakshari', 'Sa re ga ma...', 'Boogie Woogie', *Get Gorgeous*, including one called *Super Moms* on the Malayalam Amritha channel, cater to a diversity of talents.[24]

That the media possesses the power to alter people's futures is clear today. If celebrity status is marked by having a media presence then it is clear that one either belongs to the media realm or the ordinary one. There is a symbolic boundary between the media world and the ordinary one, a boundary that contestants in such shows as *Indian Idol* re-inscribe. Such contests ensure that ordinary people from ordinary realms shift into the media world.[25] In this media world, they get a chance to garner a public validation of their self-worth. Such a chance generates both symbolic and material benefits. The only way out of the ordinary realm is to get into the media world.

It is also important to note that such contests produce a celebrity from the streets, as it were, with no connections. These are not children of film families, royalty or industrialists. These are college students, ordinary middle-class people who become celebrities precisely because of their *lack of connection* with traditional structures of power and influence. Their very ordinariness, coupled with some talent, makes them marketable, mediagenic commodities.

Reality television, such as *Big Brother* in Euro-American contexts, followed by *Survivor* and now *Celebrity Big Brother* and our own MTV's *Roadies* and *KBC* provided the stage (literally) for anybody to compete. These are 'spectacles of everyday life' (Kellner 2003: 7), where real-life events recorded for television make celebrities. It must be noted that shows like *Bigg Boss* or *Roadies* also mark the arrival and dissemination of the surveillance society, satirised in the 1998 film *The Truman Show*, where the individual's every act, movement and emotion are recorded, thus providing a spectacle of the everyday. Reality TV satisfies the voyeuristic urge in us where the everyday life of somebody else becomes our entertainment. Reality TV is also popular because there is a touch of authenticity about it, and this appeals to the audience saturated with carefully choreographed plots and special effects.

Dramatic serials such as *CID* (building on Euro-American ones such as *ER*, *NYPD Blue* and *Boston Legal*) are also popular spectacles because they tap into deep social anxieties about crime, safety and law. Aligned on the same plane as gangster flicks such as the hugely successful *Satya* (1998) and *Shootout at Lokhandwala* (2007), these transform celebrity real-life criminals in contemporary India into celefictions.

Quiztime in the 1980s, *India Mastermind*, and more glam-orously *KBC*, made quizzing a highly attractive contest. Ellis Cashmore suggests that with the proliferation of channels the information-analysis-reflection dimension of programmes was gradually replaced by amusement (Cashmore 2006: 9). There is considerable truth in the argument. Ordinary people who have only seen others on screen and in the spotlight now have a greater chance to go up there. Although none of it is untrained contest, it expands the possibility of being part of a staged spectacle surely, an innovation in entertainment. Theoretically speaking, one does not need a film connection or a celebrity family to become a celebrity now. As MTV puts it, 'they've become used to a bit of recognition (the celebrity syndrome) they loved the attention they got from the camera and crew'.[26]

Reality TV and contests are a form of *social mobility* for many people. They move from being ordinary people to rec-ognisable people, winners and photographed faces. Reality TV and such shows can be seen as a form of validation, a public recognition of their talents.

Reality TV creates celebrities based on the drama of every-day life—watching people 2⟨ ⟨7 on screen. It is assumed that in *Bigg Boss* or *Big Brother*, the phenomenal Reality TV show that set the prototype for all future shows, the people are being their true selves, which, apparently, we are all interested in. The fact that *Bigg Boss* relies upon the already present celebrity quotient of its participants—from Rahul Roy of *Aashiqui* (1990) fame to the current item-girl sensation, Rakhi Sawant, ensures that we take a greater interest in them. *Roadies* aims to make celebrities out of ordinary people, capturing their emotions, behaviour, manners and relationships for voyeuristic public consumption, by an audience that is perhaps tired of faked emotions on the film screen. The blurring of the private and public in such programmes marks a new kind of celebrity cul-ture, where being *ordinary, that is, without particular or spec-tacular talents or looks, still ensures fame by being on TV.*

Reality TV follows the same pattern as any soap opera or film. Characters are good or bad and there is always *drama*.

Situations in the *Bigg Boss* house, the tensions between Carol Gracias and Rakhi Sawant, for example, or the famous Jade Goody-Shilpa Shetty incident in UK's *Celebrity Big Brother*, ensure that such binaries of character emerge so that the public or audience is expected to vote out the bad ones.[27] The *participatory celebrity culture* of the Reality TV show where the audience contributes to the making of the celebrity. What makes the Reality TV personality or character a celebrity is the audience's assumption that this is for real. The individual on the screen is not working out of a script or storyline. Thus a celebrity is one whose deepest anxieties and emotions are supposedly captured without mediation and for us to consume. The enormous popularity of such programmes (*Big Brother* and *Survivor* were so popular in the UK that CBS promptly did its US run in 2000), suggests that the audience wants a greater dose of *reality on screen*, and this makes for a formula for potential celebrities. Is one willing to be monitored 24×7 and have ones emotions and behaviour recorded for all to see? If the answer is 'yes', then one has the chance to be a celebrity.[28]

Game shows like *KBC*, the various contests, talk shows (*NextGen*) also constitute a similar demotic turn.[29] There is something more here that gives celebrity culture an additional twist. Although the focus in talk shows or the various talent contests is apparently on the individual, the structure of the programme makes it a site of multiple intersections. The individual in the hot seat is the subject of public scrutiny through telecast, where SMS and online voting often determine her or his fortune. This makes for a *participatory celebrity culture where the individual becomes a celebrity not only through the structure of the event that she or he wins but through the audience voting for her or him.* What I want to emphasise here is not the distinctive feature of the celebrity but the *format* that constructs an individual as a celebrity. That is, the distinction once focused on the *individual* celebrity is now on the *format* that helps make a celebrity. Celebrity culture has reached a stage where it transforms the processes through which celebrities are made. If earlier game winners and the most talented were victorious, now it is the most *popular*, rated by a global audience reaching for their keyboards and cell phones, who are celebrity victors.

It is not enough to have celebrities. They must be *made* through *distinctive processes* that are themselves unique and attractive. It was curious to see compere Mini Mathur, when requesting people to vote for *Indian Idol 3* competitor Smita Adhikari (13 July 2007), phrase it this way: 'If you have been impressed by Smita Adhikari's makeover, SMS...' Smita had undergone a massive makeover earlier in the contest, and both jury and studio audience seemed happy with her new avatar. Here the narrative of *Indian Idol* shifts, as we have already noted in Chapter 2, from raw talent to the willingness to be groomed and to accept advice from the industry.

So then, is the contest about makeovers or singing talents? Is it that Smita Adhikari must appeal to the eye, and this is not an isolated case, everybody comments on the contestant's *looks*, rather than to the ear? And, in any case, why is it that the programme's opening shots show only a male body, raising arms in triumph, in silhouette?[30] As for the audience voting from all over the country, it is not enough to be talented, it is important to be *liked* and *appreciated* by an audience *outside* the game's format. Hence Mini Mathur's exhortation: 'Viewers, please think and vote'!

Thus public voting to decide on winners is a unique format that leaves the celebrity text far more open than before. Albert Almeida, the head of Sony Entertainment Television, admitted that the thin response to *Indian Idol 2* inspired them to make changes in the format. Almeida said: 'We're making changes in the format...we have made changes to surprise viewers to make the show a lot more engaging' (Almeida 2007: 72). As a result there are mobile phone auditions. The emphasis is on more interesting *formats* here, as we can see. The point is that talent contests are also, basically, *entertainments*, even as they seek celebrities.

There is nothing particularly Indian about *Indian Idol*, except for its contestants' nationality. In the global culture market, and with the possibilities of overseas programmes, sales and shows, *each contestant is modelled as any other international pop icon or star rather than as anything distinctively Indian.*

Magazines like *Society* report on ordinary people who have achieved something unique. For instance, Leela Bordia is not the usual kind of fashionable celebrity. However, this woman won the National Award for Outstanding Export Performance in 1993–1996 and 1998–2003. Working out of Kolkata, Bordia sells Rajasthan's famous blue pottery. A person otherwise out of the limelight, Bordia becomes the face of the ordinary-turned-celebrity with coverage in mass media. *Society* magazine carried a piece on her in its May 2007 issue.

Another mode, a less comforting or pleasing one, of becoming a celebrity is as a survivor or victim of a disaster. These figures are celetoids. *Short term but hyper-visible* figures, who are witnesses to or survivors of a bomb blast, victims of massacres, a particularly well known criminal case that generates a face for TV and newspapers, are interviewed by various TV channels. In the recent past we have a few such celetoids—Minal Panchal and Professor Loganathan, the two Indians killed in the Virginia Tech shootout of April 2007. *The Hindu* showed a framed photograph of Minal and a news report of a memorial meeting at Mumbai's Rizvi College of which she was an alumnus.[31] There were regular news reports about the arrangements being made for Professor Loganathan's family to reach Virginia. Other victims, such as Pakistan's Mukhtar or Mukhtaran Mai, gang-raped as a form of honour-revenge, became the toast of celebrity circuits in the USA and Europe, winning a host of awards. Ironically, even Mukhtar Mai was appropriated by the fashion-consumer circuit when *Glamour Magazine* declared her the 'Glamour Woman of the Year' in 2005.[32]

Celetoids are also those linked with transgression, scandal and notoriety. The accused in the Nithari killings (Moninder

Singh Pandher), those in the eye of a scam like the Member of Parliament Babubhai Katara are celetoids. Notoriety is also as spectacular as any other form of celebrification because it attracts, at least briefly, a hyper-visibility in the global media. They are subjects of talk shows, newspaper editorials, letters to the editor, cartoons and tabloid inquiry. They remain in the public eye for a brief period, to resurface occasionally. Each of these constitutes a spectacle in celebrity culture.

Performance, Spectacle, Anti-Spectacle

As I write this, the Concert for Diana on 1 July 2007 is live on Star World from Wembley (London). It was organised by the princes William and Harry, with star performers like Elton John, Duran Duran and Nelly Furtado. The 'People's Princess' would have been 46 if she were alive. The massive crowds, with their banners ('Diana: Queen of our Hearts Forever'), demonstrated two things: the staying power of even a dead celebrity, and the perpetual linkage of celebrity culture with spectacle.[33] Central to the celebrity's popularity is visibility. In many cases this visibility is tied to their original domains.

The work of artists and illusionists like the celebrity magicians P.C. Sorcar, Jadugar Anand and Akash in India and the illusionist David Blaine in England constitutes spectacular performance. On 14 May 2007, newspapers in Hyderabad reported how Mr Akash, the son of the famous Jadugar Anand was 'handcuffed, shackled, sealed in a sack, locked in a wooden box' and lowered into the Hussain Sagar lake, only to have him escape in 15 seconds, breaking his father's 37-year-old record.[34] David Blaine in September 2003 sealed himself in a glass sphere hung over the Tower Bridge in London, to try and live for 44 days without food or water. Both of these are event television, involving extensive visibility and multimedia coverage.[35] The event is often accompanied by commentary, reportage across media and commercial value.

What do such performances and spectacles have to do with celebrity culture?

These performances attract enormous media and public attention and provide visibility, thereby fulfilling one of the key requirements of celebrity culture. Second, there is a large commercial profit to be made from telecasts, sponsors and promotional campaigns. Yet what makes the performances of Akash and Blaine celebrity material is the theme of physicality.

We have already noted how celebrity culture is linked to fashion and the body. The feat of escaping from inside a box when shackled or starving oneself is a related aspect of celebrity culture, but one that often escapes attention. It is the *potential* risk to the performer's body and life that makes it a celebrity event. A corresponding event would be the injuries suffered by film stars during their shooting and the injuries that dog sport stars.[36] Whether illusion or reality (Blaine's were live events, enhancing his reputation as that of an illusionist), the performance shows the body as being subject to severe trauma and life-endangering risk. It makes *the body of the performer a celebrity body for having endured and survived.*

The presence of the crowds around Akash or Blaine lends the event its air of both *liveness* and intimacy. The noise and the spectacle generates the air of celebrity, a common feature during film shootings, as we know in India. But more significantly, *the crowds constitute the audience of ordinary people from whom the performer stands apart—as the celebrity, the extraordinary individual.* It is theatre of a live kind, and one that is dramatic for its dangers that are visible at close quarters and not on screen mediated by music and settings.[37]

Celebrity spectacles also result from a public individual shifting across domains. In India, one of the finest examples of a celebrity utilising expertise from one domain in another was M.G. Ramachandran. A swash-buckling hero in Tamil films, MGR, as he was popularly known, was a cult figure in the state when he shifted to politics. Winning elections and becoming Chief Minister, MGR, with the trademark dark glasses, became the forerunner to Ronald Reagan and Arnold Schwarzenegger in the USA and N.T. Rama Rao in India. N.T. Rama Rao, like MGR, came to politics from films. Known for his high-flown speeches especially in mythologicals, NTR adopted the same, highly dramatic form of speechifying on his tours and on television. Schwarzenegger is reported to have used his famous 'I'll be back' lines from the *Terminator* films during his election campaign. MGR and NTR embody another element of celebrity spectacle: performance and the appropriation of the language, codes and mannerisms of one domain by and into another.

We see some kind of *celebrity crossover* when Amitabh Bachchan or Tendulkar do propaganda roles in public interest; a kind of democratisation of the celebrity audience, but also the suggestion of celebrity social responsibility. Amitabh Bachchan's famous voice (an interesting example of a celebrity that relies as much on the aural as the visual) exhorted people to administer polio vaccine to their children. Sachin Tendulkar participated in a Batsman Fitness Camp in Bangalore in June 2007 where a special audience of physically challenged children was treated to an interaction with the stars.[38]

Such performances, it could be argued, raised the celebrity *above* the public—a position of authority from where decisions made could affect millions. From the film, with its financial and cultural economy, to the public sphere, the celebrity spectacle of electioneering, cabinet meetings, parades and public appearances as CM the celebrity has risen. They acquire a different aura through this kind of performance.

Chris Rojek locates a shamanic *magic* in celebrity culture, an argument that fits figures like MGR and NTR very well. Rojek suggests that action film stars (Harrison Ford, Bruce Willis, Pierce Brosnan) are required to perform magical feats on screen. Sports stars like Tiger Woods or Venus Williams are expected to do the same on the sports field (Rojek 2001: 77).

Both MGR and NTR imported their exotic, magical roles from the mythological film into the political arena. The Angry Young Man, Amitabh Bachchan, also tried his hand at it. Jayaprada and Vijayshanti, the Telugu film actresses and Jayalalitha from Tamil films, are crowd-pullers in the political rally, just as they exerted a similar magic on the screen. The film star serves to weave a spell, on screen or off it. This is the first *role* of the celebrity actor-turned-politician.[39] But they are also expected to live those roles out in real life: be good, brave and honest, and change society, roles they had played dozens of times on screen.

Other magical elements include the actor-turned-politician's unaging appearance. The careful attention to the body seems to resist decay and even death. Like the gods they once played, MGR and NTR's groomed appearances in public spaces offered the suggestion of their immortality! The immortality of the screen role, preserved in multiple media forms long after the film is screened, ensures, it could be argued, their immortality in the public sphere. And this magic is what the celebrity actors capitalised on.

One version of the television spectacle is the talk show, and not always of the Oprah Winfrey kind. Astrology, parenting, health and advice, celebrity talk shows, programmes like *Janata ki Adalat*, which ran for a record eight years and catapulted Rajat Sarma into the realm of television celebrities, are all part of the new media landscape that attempts to create a new public space where ordinary people and celebrities can both express their opinions, promote products, confess to their flaws and fears and offer advice. News readers such as Prannoy Roy, Rajdeep Sardesai and Barkha Dutt are celebrities in their own right, as their performances on the TV screen as not just news readers but as opinion-shapers become household names. Barkha Dutt even inspired a movie role—Preity Zinta's in Farhan Akhtar's *Lakshya* (2004).

These are heavily *mediatised* performances, even when they are live. Spectacle on television is always the effect of the mass media. Live telecasts of performances like that of magicians (Akash) or street theatre, and made available for instant replay, blur the distinction between live and mediated performance when the *media intrudes into the live performance itself.*

Celebrity culture thrives on this aspect: even when individuals in *Bigg Boss* are live they are mediated, performances circulated on TV as audio and video and through other forms of technological reproduction. Videos of the episodes are available on the website for repeated viewing, if one so desires. Therefore, it is not possible to separate live performance from mediated performance.[40]

Talk shows with studio audiences are a prominent feature on western television and is a phenomenon rapidly catching up in India. In March 2007 NDTV launched *NextGen*, with Amitabh's daughter, Shweta Nanda as compere. Talk shows are not simply about people conversing on various topics. It entails a commodification of the audience. The audience markets goods and ideas to itself. The people in the audience learn to vote for certain beliefs, and disseminate certain codes of taste, looks, talents and popularity. They espouse the ideology of achievement, talent, merit, financial success and consumerism—what I have termed meritocratic capitalism. Furthermore, the advertisers buy access to these audiences (*NextGen* targets professionals under 40).

Astrology and medical talk shows with phone-in queries, now common to all channels, are also increasingly a part of celebrity culture. Doctors and palmists are now celebrity TV personalities with a wider audience than they ever had. Then there are exercise and fitness specialists and the yoga exponents (Ramdev Baba). Such shows create a different kind of celebrity. The *expert* and a new culture, that of *expertise*. Psychiatrists and counsellors believe they competent to listen to and advise people on their private lives. Phone-in services enable the sufferer to outline her or his symptoms and the doctor-expert on television offers advice, where both the symptoms of the voice-only patient and the cure are telecast to large audiences.

The talk show is also linked here to the *culture of consumption via the medium of expert knowledge* whether it is fashion, health, medical advice, spirituality, family matters or home furnishings. These talk shows cater to the anxieties of the society, and offer possible solutions, many of which take the form of buyable products ranging from medicines to exercise cycles.[41] Expert celebrities sell us particular medication, goods or self-help products under the label of advice. This form of sales pitch is one step removed from outright promotional work, but achieves the same results—consumerism. If promotional culture unabashedly promotes products via film or sports celebrities, talk shows and expert shows do the same via the culture of expert knowledge. Experts in fact come in on a regular basis as advisers on shows like *Get Gorgeous* (on channel V) or as members of the jury. What we see is a new cult of the *expert celebrity* as opposed to the *star celebrity*.

Another significant kind of celebrity spectacle is achieved by celebrity activists. Medha Patkar, Arundhati Roy, Asma Jehangir (the civil liberties lawyer in Pakistan) and organisations like Greenpeace also work with the media but are not seeking political power. Greenpeace, however, does have representation in some parliaments around the world. This is another kind of celebrity politician, one who is an activist, effectively uses the media and intervenes in social debates. They are able to procure audiences like any celebrity and political attention, even if their domain is the urban populace.

Spectacle and performance, however, is not restricted to celebrity figures alone. As we have seen in the previous chapter, national events, like the Republic Day parade, the Red Fort celebrations on 15 August, are also spectacles and elaborately choreographed performances. Another kind of celebrity spectacle is also common today. The Gulf War transformed our television screens into a medium of real-time horror with the live footages of raids and battles.[42] The 'war on terror' and in Iraq used embedded journalists who converted the war into photo-ops. Finally, the visuals from Abu Ghraib generated a whole new, tragic celebrity spectacle for the new millennium.

The 'war on terror' was a visual spectacle like its predecessor, the Gulf War. Studies of the media-entertainment complex's links with the war have explored the extraordinary control and dissemination over the spectacle.

I shift the scene of the debate away from film stars and India to Abu Ghraib because, along with the cell phone movie clip of Saddam's execution, the visuals of prisoner abuse have offered a challenge to the control of celebrity spectacle as never before. Further, the electronic globalisation of the world reassigns geographies of celebrities and spectacles who now are no longer restricted to countries and cultures.

Abu Ghraib marks a celebrity event by virtue of its sheer horror. What is important to note here is that these are visuals that become celebrity visuals because they were not meant to be seen. I propose the term *anti-spectacle* to refer to those visuals that become famous precisely by their characteristic of 'not-meant-to-be-seen'. Nicholas Mirzoeff's (2006: 23) description of the Abu Ghraib visuals as being invisible because the media and the general public had accepted that they had no right to see these images, summarises what I am calling the *celebrity anti-spectacle*. This argument about celebrity anti-spectacle can also be applied to Saddam's execution, recorded on a mobile phone camera by one of those present.

As another, more local form of anti-spectacle, we can think of ministers caught dozing in meetings or in Parliament, Lalu Yadav getting a hair-cut, or a film star performing something mundane or even indiscreet. The famous Shahid Kapur-Kareena kiss, the gossip magazines' brief mentions of stars being seen together in restaurants; or, more recently, Prince Harry kissing his girl friend at the July 2007 Concert for Diana, even though, surely, Harry knew that at least a dozen cameras were dedicated to recording every moment of his presence. These again are not meant to be seen. These are celebrity anti-spectacles because they escape the state control over public spectacles. The shot of a minister sleeping at a public function is not what the government wants telecast, but it gets front page coverage anyway. These resist monolithic celebrity spectacles and meanings. As opposed to the theatrical, controlled visual production of the media house or the state, we have the shaky, grainy, awkward visual of the accident.

A qualification is perhaps in order. Some of what I am calling celebrity anti-spectacles are not necessarily about celebrity faces or people. There are often sideshows and visual asides to grand, mediated spectacles that achieve brief hyper-visibility in newspapers and television by virtue of their very ordinariness, or general invisibility. These are not *spectacular*, but that does not mean they are any *less as* spectacles. Side-lights of grand spectacles of Independence Day celebrations constitute celebrity anti-spectacle even when they do not involve recognisable faces. A labourer toiling in the fields, the rickshaw puller on the road—images that are very common in newspapers today—shot by amateurs with handy-cams, mobile phone cameras, and often by accident—these are fine examples of the other side of celebrity spectacle. In an age where there is increasing corporate media control over spectacles and their dissemination these visual texts constitute a resistance to such control. What I am calling anti-spectacle is not an evaluation of the technological apparatus but rather a descriptive of its accidental, amateur or even politically subversive nature.

Performance, Politics and Power

All celebrities possess a certain amount of power. In the case of celebrity politicians the link between celebrity and power is very clear. The entertainer, who has thus far achieved power in the cultural realm, now adds politics to the repertoire. The politician, in a related fashion, is able to harness the mediums of representation and performance to generate support.

Performance and the Political

The celebrity politician, from MGR to Lalu Yadav, is also a performer. Celebrity politicians whose backgrounds are in movies or show business extend their performance from stage or screen to the political arena. As John Street's work on political celebrities has demonstrated (2004), many political leaders appropriate, with great effect, the mechanisms of popular culture, folk culture and local imagery.

MGR and NTR's success in politics is an interesting case of what could be called *masquerade celebrity*. The *roles* essayed become celebrities themselves. The film star who essays the *role* of a politician or king or god suddenly becomes all these as a Chief Minister. MGR and NTR were both massive crowd-pulling spectacles in and of themselves. Iconic figures in the film industry, they had cult followings in their respective states. Their public appearances were extremely well attended and they performed.

What MGR and NTR did was to perform a masquerade, a reversal of the propaganda roles played by entertainers and sports stars. They moved into the territory marked out by politicians. Having played the hero in films dozens of times as the saviour, the do-gooder, the villain-basher, the god, they entered politics as 'good' celebrities, albeit in their film *roles*. They subverted the domain of politics by converting election-eering, the legislature and the public appearances, into theatre. Icons of popular culture, specifically Hindu culture, were used effectively to gather attention.[43] They occupied and performed a *role* previously played by professional politicians, a masquerade celebrity when the star from a film played one more role, this time a more determinate, influential one. They introduced themselves into an aspect of the public sphere—of which culture (such as film) is one—and became celebrity politicians. This is *masquerade celebrity* because the fake and the counterfeit (the film *roles* played by MGR and NTR) become the real. The line between role-playing or performance on screen and in 'real life' breaks down. The superimposition of the film role upon the face and office of the chief minister is an extraordinary example of the post-modern play of real versus artifice. In this case, it is hard to distinguish between the two—politics becomes an extension of entertainment.

It could be argued that the entertainer turned politician trivializes politics and political representation. However, following Street's argument (2004), it is possible to see celebrity politicians as *extending the domains of democratic represen-tation*. The celebrity is a representative of the people's aspira-tions, hopes and desires. They could, therefore, be said to speak for the people. Furthermore, they also have a certain amount of affective capacity (Street 2004: 448), pulling crowds, getting them to respond and being able to open the public space. This is *celebrity power*.

Celebrity politicians also include activists who may not be seeking political office. Medha Patkar and Arundhati Roy in the Narmada anti-dam movement, entertainers like Richard Gere or Jane Fonda who take up causes (Amitabh Bachchan for polio vaccinations is a famous instance) also extend the semantic scope of the term political—the people take their cue from and form opinions because of celebrity glamour and power—what Marks and Fischer have termed *simulating consent* (Marks and Fischer 2002).

The celebrity becomes, in such cases (and Patkar is an excel-lent example of this), the embodiment of a people's suffering, opinions, aspirations and political demands. In this sense, the celebrity functions as a crucial component of the practices of democratic representation because they re-invigorate public space and civil society.

Celebrity power here is about *agency*, the ability to raise consciousness, open up public spaces, generate debates and embody people's ambitions: Vivek Oberoi working for tsunami victims, Amitav Ghosh writing about them, Shabana Azmi and others filing petitions. These are also performances in the sense that they are deliberate and conscious attempts to focus media attention upon certain issues and perhaps influence political-administrative decisions. The celebrity who possesses consid-erable agency, especially over the media and representation, is here functioning as a medium through which public opinion can be focussed and articulated. They become cultural elites who are in a position to expand audiences, and thus serve an important political function.[44]

The realm of the political here includes such diverse areas as public health, environmental concerns, welfare and minority emancipation. When celebrities speak for people or causes, they achieve a certain measure of politically-edged media exposure for those people or causes. Examples include Shabana Azmi and Arundhati Roy speaking for minorities. It makes for a degree of democratisation when the celebrity opens up the space of the debate precisely by virtue of being a celebrity. They expand the audiences for the debates far beyond the confines of the parliament when they take to the streets or appear on TV. In short, they generate a certain critical attention to issues, especially those in which they possess legitimate standing. Thus the interventions of celebrity authors regarding the censorship or harassment of Salman Rushdie or Taslima Nasreen or about the fine arts exhibition at MS University (Baroda, May 2007) are *political* interventions. The celebrity author uses the location of her or his domain to address larger issues of freedom of speech, secularism and the scope of the literary, all of which have political dimensions and consequences, at least in the case of Nasreen and Rushdie.

Celebrity agency demands considerable mediated presence in public space. Film celebrities come with a certain amount of media presence and politicians are increasingly media savvy. Everything about Lalu Yadav attracts media attention, P. Chidambaram and Manmohan Singh are both mediagenic personalities. Indira Gandhi radiated power, and Rajiv Gandhi exuded charm. Adolf Hitler held audiences spellbound. Televangelists and experts on TV, from Paul Dinakaran to Ramdev Baba, generate enormous audience responses. Celebrity agency depends on such a performance.

Charisma and Celebrity

Charisma, a term often used to describe celebrities and leaders today, originally referred to gifts of divine grace that manifest as prophecy or healing. It now refers to exceptional people and their traits.

All celebrities, whether politicians in power or activists commanding the attention of thousands, possess charisma. Roger Eatwell's theorisation of the working of charisma is a useful tool to analyse celebrity power (Eatwell 2006). The 'charismatic bond' (Eatwell 2006: 142) enables the celebrity to command an audience, whom she or he can persuade to accept her or his point of view. This bond is built through particular modes.

Powerful leaders often present a vision. Whether it is Hitler's vision of a master race or Abdul Kalam's vision of a scientifically advanced India, all leaders offer the people a programme of action driven by a set of ideals and ideas. Political manifestoes of parties and pre-election speeches by leaders often seek to project a clear idea of their plans for the country and the people. Martin Luther King Jr.'s speech 'I have a dream' is precisely this kind of a vision that enables the charismatic bond. Celebrities being interviewed on TV often speak of their ideas for future projects, their plans for the next film, serial or business venture. The 'I-hope-to' or 'I-want-to' line common to celebrity interviews and personal descriptions serve this purpose of projecting a vision. For the celebrity's charisma to develop, this vision must be something the audience identifies with, and treats as relevant, useful and worth following.

Charismatic leaders work by showing themselves to be like one of the people. A common ploy here is to identify themselves as belonging to the people. From Gandhi to Mayawati, leaders have constantly tried to mix with the people. Photographs of leaders handling babies, talking to old men or women or using a farm implement are commonplace in newspapers. This enables the population to identify with the dominant and powerful leader. In fact, the leader's charisma has a *symbiotic relationship with the people*. When they see her or him in the flesh, as an ordinary man or woman it reiterates the hierarchy—the leader who is at the top of the social structure has descended to earth and has mixed with the ordinary folks. A 'mahatma' who is like one of us asks that we respond precisely in that awe-struck way—this is the charisma of the leader who slums it in the city or rural India.

The personal magnetism of the leader is, of course, a crucial element in the charismatic bond. Fans and mesmerised audiences are common features of all charismatic bonds. People reaching out to touch SRK or waiting for hours to catch a glimpse of a leader know the difference between themselves (the audience) and the celebrity they await. Yet the personal magnetism and the pull of the positional celebrities is such that crowds put themselves through enormous trouble to see them.

Television has brought charisma into the drawing room. Aman Varma, Smriti Irani, and former film stars like Kiran Kumar and Neena Gupta are stars created, or resurrected in the case of Kumar and Gupta, by the television medium. Televangelists and TV celebrities like Paul Dinakaran, Sri Sri Ravi Sankar and Ramdev Baba possess what David Diekema has identified as a *mediated charisma* (Diekema 1991). Each one of the television celebrities listed above possesses considerable personal charm and exudes power. What is however important to note is that much of this charm and power proceeds from a heavily mediated context. They come to us from very carefully staged performances, the conversations, crowds and the media. Mediated charisma also refers to the institutional contexts from which each of these speak—evangelical Christianity, yoga and Hindu philosophy. Their magnetism is partly the result of the power of these institutional or structural contexts out of which they function, but for which they serve as the focalising point. They possess agency not only as individual celebrities but as celebrities who represent something more—a way of life, a philosophy or an institution.

Charismatic leaders and televangelists emerge in particular social contexts. An unstable society revives cults and assorted faiths and provides even charismatic leaders with what Eatwell calls *cultural legitimation* (Eatwell 2006: 149–50). A socio-economic crisis or political instability causes the people to yearn for, and eventually 'discover' a strong leader. The leader asserts power and the activist commands attention because the contexts allow, even demand, they act this way. Charisma is thus a *context-bound feature*, where social crises throw up celebrities who then offer visions and alternatives to the current situation. The charismatic appeal of specific types, therefore, is symptomatic of a cultural anxiety or social tension (Dyer 2002: 30–2). Hitler's charisma, for example, was fuelled by the anxieties of the German people after the disastrous First World War.

The televangelist is the focal actor who also articulates the needs, concerns and anxieties of the crowds she or he addresses, and this includes the audience the speaker never sees—the ones watching her or him on TV. Through their direct communication with the audience, humour and conversational style, they address the individual rather than the collective. This is charisma too, and the ability to convey the impression that the speaker is addressing you and you alone is what Diekema terms the illusion of intimacy (1991).

The charismatic televangelist also commands attention by appealing to a common and shared past. Ramdev Baba's references to Indian traditions constitute an appeal to the common past of his audiences. Whether it is Christianity or Hinduism, this appeal to a shared past ensures a bond between the leader or visionary and her or his audience. This is further strengthened by appealing to a common enemy or demonic Other. In most cases, the political leader demonises another country or the opposition. Indira Gandhi, one of the most charismatic leaders in post-independence India, constructed an entire mythography of the 'foreign hand' in the 1970s and early 1980s. In the case of Ramdev Baba it is the MNC and Western capitalist modernity that comes in for demonisation.

The charismatic leader, argues Diekema, presents 'an alternative to existing tensions and crises' (Diekema 1991). Ramdev Baba offers yoga, Sri Sri Ravi Shankar offers *sudarshan kriya* and Paul Dinakaran offers Christianity as solutions to present-day crises, both individual and collective. Their vision suggests ways out of what is often perceived as a crisis. Corruption, immorality, deviance, poor health, depression and psychological disorders, religious and communal tensions are all seen as crises to be resolved. Central to the charismatic celebrity's power is one such process of name-calling—identifying the demons, crises and tensions is a first step before offering a patented solution. The power of the celebrity here lies in their ability to convert large audiences into their ways of perceiving the world. With the charismatic bond, the celebrity ensures an audience to work through an agenda of social change. The agency of the celebrity builds on such a performance and bond and affects two forms of relations.

The Affective and the Rational

David Marshall has argued that political celebrities work through a dualism, of affective relations/responses and rationalisation (Marshall 1997: 204–5). Leaders and celebrities ensure that the audience makes an affective investment in them. Political leaders often appeal to the emotions of the people, even as they discuss a social issue. Here it is not the issue that is at stake as much as the emotional responses it or the leader provokes. Thus, when Arjun Singh discussed the reservation issue in 2006–2007, what it achieved was emotional outbursts, dismay and anger with little scope for a rational debate because, as the language of the newspapers put it 'it hurts sentiments'. The debate swerves away from rational dialogue to melodrama and hysteria. This is the affective function of a celebrity. When Arundhati Roy writes about Pokhran or Narmada, she frequently takes recourse to the language of excessive drama. Electioneering speeches are frequently attempts to sway people via an appeal to sentiment. Appeals to caste, regional, linguistic and dynastic affiliations are appeals to the emotional component of the relationship between the leader and the audience.

Thus the 1999 general elections, for example, revolved around the deeply emotional issue of the 'videshi bahu' (foreign daughter-in-law), Sonia Gandhi. As Uwe Skoda (2004) has argued, Sonia Gandhi's foreign origins were highlighted and contrasted, at least in Bellary, Karnataka, with the BJP candidate, Sushma Swaraj who was 'swadeshi beti' (Indian daughter) in a contest that was primarily emotional rather than political. In fact, and this is my point, *it is within the realm of the emotional that contemporary political celebrities work their agency*. Sonia, as the widow of a former, well-loved prime minister, worked at sympathy. She had after all lost her husband to India. Sushma Swaraj played up the native daughter angle. So what if Sonia had lost her husband, she was still a European. The affective investment audiences make in their celebrities often determine the rationalised process of elections and political power. Sonia was the unfamiliar or distant European leader whose connections were with India's most famous political family. She was thus rendered (Sonia won the elections, beating Sushma Swaraj by a considerable margin) both familiar *and* familial in the rhetoric of the daughter-in-law/daughter of the campaigns—a key feature of celebrities if they wish to acquire power (Marshall 1997: 217).

Political processes are supposedly rationalisations. Their mechanisms have no room for emotions, and work with statistics and geographies. Yet the formulation of policies, manifestoes and electioneering by political leaders works more at the level of the affective than the rational. It is here that celebrity culture's political angle becomes most complicated. The celebrity leader's agency is, surely, political. Yet *the route to the rational-political lies through the affective*. A leader who cannot appeal to and grasp the affective component of her or his constituency does not win. Political rationality is thus built on an affective function. This dualism is the source of the celebrity's agency and power.

Celebrities thus exert considerable power through their performances. The spectacle of aestheticized, fashionable or charismatic celebrity performance generates special bonds with the audience, even when the performance is of something unsavoury or which defies the acceptable norms of that culture. Scandals, which are performances of this type, are also spectacles and integral to celebrity culture, as we shall see next.

Notes

1. 'Hockey Fever at Premiere of Chak De India', *The Asian Today*, 10 August 2007. Available online at http://www.theasiantoday.com/article.aspx?articleId=489 (downloaded on 27 January 2008). I am grateful to Anna Kurian for drawing my attention to this news item. I am grateful to Anna Kurian for drawing my attention to this news item.

2. 'Not Fashionable', *The Times of India*, 1 September 2007. Available online at http://timesofindia.indiatimes.com/Entertainment/Not_fashionable_/rssarticleshow/2355201.cms (downloaded on 27 January 2008).

3. See, for example, Feasey (2006).

4. However, the fashion model body, usually wafer-thin and anorexic, has been at the centre of controversy recently. Critics of beauty contests have argued that thin fashion models send out the wrong messages to teens, who proceed to starve themselves to attain the levels of thinness seen on screen. See Bordo (1990) and Botta (1999). For an account of the debates see, Dwyer (2004).

5. http://www.apunkachoice.com/scoop/bollywood/20060401-0.html (downloaded on 20 May 2007).

6. http://www.peacockcouture.com/india.htm.

7. *Filmfare* (2007), p. 54. There were debates about why certain people were not invited to the celebrity wedding (*Deccan Chronicle* [2007], p. 21 and 23) and photographs in major newspapers (*Deccan Chronicle* [2007]).

8. *Filmfare*, April 2007, p. 54.

9. *Filmfare*, April 2007, p. 6.

10. *Filmfare*, April 2007, p. 6.

11. *Filmfare*, April 2007, p. 110.

12. *Filmfare*, May 2007, pp. 36–8.

13. http://www.despardes.com/Fashion/news/nov04/best-worst-dresses-nov13.html (downloaded on 25 May 2007).

14. It also does other kinds of homogenisation. For example, when identifying celebrities, some commentaries often pinpoint designations, family names and professions. In other cases we see only generic identities. Thus in *Hello!* (November 2007) in a coverage of the BBC

India dinner after identifying 'Italian model actress Alessia Piovan', various BBC officials we have '*Asian* actress Shu Qi' (130, emphasis added).

15. http://www.fibre2fashion.com/news/fashion-news/newsdetails (downloaded on 26 May 2007).
16. 'Celeb Tips', *Deccan Chronicle*, 2 July 2007, p. 26.
17. 'Spears May Not Get her Kids' Custody', *The Times of India*, 8 September 2007. Available online at http://timesofindia. indiatimes.com/International_Buzz/Spears_may_not_get_her_ kids_custody/articleshow/2376890.cms (downloaded on 27 January 2008).
18. According to Garry Whannel, there appears to be an intrinsic contextual link between the discourse and representation of the 'hard' sporting body and the cult of the equally hard action hero in Hollywood: *Rambo, Die Hard, Terminator, Lethal Weapon, Speed*. The invincible (male) body of these films might possibly be a correlate to the fit male body of the sports stars (Whannel, pp. 68–70). It is not uncommon to see Salman Khan in sports gear or Sunny Deol exercising in their films. Tendulkar's ads frequently show him in sports gear. Newspapers carry photographs of cricketers—mostly cricketers, Dhanraj Pillai has not been thus photographed!—at training camps, working out.
19. http://www.despardes.com/Fashion/news/2006/20060401-wardrobe-malfunction-laksme.html (downloaded on 25 May 2007).
20. *Hello!*, April 2007, p. 120.
21. Such a paradoxical encounter of the intimate and the stranger calls for special kinds of moral order (see Ferris 2004).
22. Graeme Turner proposes the demotic turn in celebrity culture where otherwise marginalized citizens now have access to media representation. See Turner (2004: 82–6).
23. *Indian Idol 1* was a massive success, and Abhijeet Sawant soon cut an album. But *Indian Idol 2* and its winner, Sandeep Acharya, received only a lukewarm response. For the third edition they brought in as jury Javed Akhtar, Udit Narayan, Alisha Chinai and Anu Malik. Its auditions also went to the UK to tap Indian talents there.
24. To take just one regional language television as example, we can still a formidable list of contests: Asianet has *Star Singer, Superstar Junior, Minnum Tārum*, Asianet Plus has *Smile Please Mimicry Star* and *Screen Test*, Amrita has *Super Mom, Super Star Global* and *Super Star*, Kairali has *Gandharva*.
25. The reverse also happens when the media enters the ordinary world of the passer-by to telecast the everyday on the screen.
26. http://www.mtvindia.com/mtv/mymtv/shows/roadies/epguide. php (downloaded on 26 March 2007).

27. A new racism incident has broken out on the other version, *Big Brother*. Emily Parr was asked by Channel 4 to leave the programme after an alleged racist remark against Charley Uchea. See Conlan, 2007.

28. Popularity polls, voting, messages and letters to stars and celebrities also exemplify participatory celebrity culture. For example, *Filmfare*-Yahoo! ran a poll dealing with movie business. The results of the polls and the very act of voting were described as 'catalysts that will change the colour, texture and power of the strong potion that is the movie business' (*Filmfare*, July 2007, p. 74). The readers/ people were asked questions about their favourite stars, questions that ranged from 'which couple is most likely to tie the knot in 2007' to 'which of these actresses would you like to see opposite Abhishek Bachchan'.

29. Quiz programmes are not necessarily neutral or pure entertainment. A study of *Who Wants to be a Millionaire?*' across USA, Western Europe (Poland, Germany, Russia, Italy), Israel and Saudi Arabia revealed interesting differences. There exists a 'knowledge hierarchy' in specific formats of the show, as discerned from an analysis of 1888 questions collected from 65 programmes. In the USA there was a high percentage of questions on light entertainment and a low on language questions. In Europe and Saudi Arabia it was the reverse. East Europe and Saudi had higher number of questions from history and little from light entertainment. For this, what I take to be a path-breaking study, see Hetsroni, 2005.

30. *The Hindu*, in an objectionably titled and badly written a feature on Indian chess wizard Koneru Humpy, focused on her *makeover*—once again suggesting the centrality of looks and personality to celebrity culture, no matter that Humpy's talents are in an entirely different field (Sridharan, 2007).

31. *The Hindu*, 20 April 2007.

32. See an update at http://www.glamour.com/news/listings/articles/2006/10/30/mukhtarmaiupdate (downloaded on 17 September 2007).

33. For a study of the making of Diana as a cultural icon see Davies (2001).

34. See *The Hindu*, 14 May 2007 and *Deccan Chronicle*, 14 May 2007, p. 21. Akash is now preparing to ride a motorcycle blindfolded.

35. Blaine's feat—suspended after 20 days—was streamed live, 24×7, on Channel 4's broadband. Blaine has several such performances to his credit: being buried alive under the streets (1999), encased in a block of ice (2000) and staying atop a 100-foot pole with no support for 36 hours (2002).

36. Building on such risk we have Reality TV such as *Survivor*.

37. For a reading of the traumatised body as spectacle in Blaine's performance see Biressi (2004).
38. *Deccan Chronicle*, 13 June 2007, p. 20.
39. Recognising the significance of celebrity culture in a country's popular culture and politics, the Norman Lear Centre (University of Southern California Annenberg School for Communication) has, since 2000, under the co-directorship of Leo Braudy (author of *The Frenzy of Renown*) run a seminar on 'Celebrity, Politics, Public Life'.
40. On 'liveness' in contemporary performance see Auslander (1999).
41. This culture of expert knowledge can also be linked to the number of publications titled '50 ways to ...' or 'do ... in 6 easy steps', created by so-called experts in specific fields.
42. See, for example, Gray, 1997.
43. A parallel from another culture and time exists. In 1966 John Lennon declared that the Beatles were more famous than Jesus Christ—a statement that worked the idea of celebrity deification both ways: Christ as celebrity and the celebrity as God. Extending on this theme, the rock opera *Jesus Christ Superstar*, was released in 1970 and became a Broadway show in 1973. See Fox (2006).
44. However, it is more than possible that celebrities provide distraction from the main cause by with their considerable glamour quotient. Their 'representative' character in social movements, argue Meyer and Gamson (1995), is questionable too.

4

Star Spotting: Celebrity and Scandal

Paris Hilton being arrested just makes her more famous.
> – Michael Levine, publicist
> (Levine 2006)

In our age of the scandalisation of public life the media suffers from an overload of film stars, sports personalities, politicians and industrialists, that is, celebrities, caught in socially unacceptable situations. Debates about the collapse of values in public life are often triggered by such scandals as rave parties of college students,[1] sports stars and their misdeeds and, to much lesser degree (understandably), politicians and their corruption. Stars are, however, always spotted—identified with and maligned, admired and abused. Stars are scarred.

Is it possible to be a celebrity without a scandal attached? Is a celebrity without the faintest whiff of scandal worth a newspaper's Page 3 at all? Indeed, as Roger Wilkes points out, it is the legitimisation of scandal and celebrity watching by even respectable newspapers that enables the establishment of gossip as a socially acceptable genre (Wilkes 2002: 9).

And why are we interested in reading about celebrity affairs, bankruptcy, violence or madness? Why should we care whether a celebrity has been arrested for drunken driving when dozens of ordinary road users across the country get into the same situation everyday?

Celebrity and scandal are closely linked, where scandal often *enhances* the celebrity quotient of the star, though long-term effects might be less cheery. In other words, even apparently negative discourses and representations of their failed marriages (practically every film star), their paedophilia (Michael Jackson), breaking the law (Salman Khan), extravagance (Victoria Beckham's shopping expeditions during the 2006 World Cup), are important to the culture of celebrity. Scandalous celebrities are arguably in greater demand than ordinary celebrities in terms of media coverage. Celebrity scandals appeal to us because, as this chapter argues, they make two, perhaps contradictory, moves simultaneously. They humanise larger-than-life figures, and they enhance the envied celebrity's larger-than-life stature as one who can indulge in behaviour, situations and acts that we ordinary people cannot. Scandal constitutes the ecology of the celebrity.

Celebrity scandal is not about celebrity lives alone, but also *scandalous events that convert particular people or events into celebrities or icons of notoriety.* Recent examples would be the Korean immigrant Cho Sueng Hui involved in the Virginia Tech shootout in April of 2007 and the Bangalore doctors suspected of terrorist attacks in the UK, in June-July of 2007.

Celebrity scandal is driven in part by the sensationalisation of news itself. TV channels and news reports seek the dramatic, the disastrous and the horrifying in a bid to capture and retain attention. Sting operations have become a recurring phenomenon, where the culprit often becomes a celebrity out of a general public sympathy for being made a victim through the journalists' operation. The recent example of the Delhi sting operation that caught a school teacher indulging in human trafficking in 2007, which subsequently proved to be a fabrication, is a case in point (Saxena 2007). When the sensational, the personal and the dramatic are staple ingredients of news itself, scandal reportage and gossip about celebrities are *extensions* of the dramatic and the sensational.

The formula for celebrity, besides financial and cultural success, hyper-visibility, power, also includes 'transgression, betrayal, restlessness and loss' (Richard de Cordova, quoted in

Holmes and Redmond 2006: 288). These are not aspects of representation or media-circulated images alone, but a logical extension of the culture of celebrity itself. I propose that part of the aura of celebrity is not simply transgression but the very idea and practice of *excess*, such as excessive drinking, scandalous deeds, wealth, power, good looks and lifestyle. The exaggerated, dramatic and hyper-visible descriptions and depictions of celebrities is linked, I suggest, to the excesses that they are expected to have.

The culture of celebrity, as we know, thrives on sustained interest in the private lives behind the public faces of the star. That is, we are curious about what they are in secret, away from the media glare. The entry into star homes that are very carefully choreographed in magazines like *Society* or *Hi!* is a legitimate access to the secret, personal space of the star. We could argue, therefore, that one of the key elements of the logic of celebrity culture is the *logic of secrecy—our* interest in *their* secrets. The perception of misdeeds when performed or committed by celebrities is considerably different. An illegality or an act that infringes social norms of morality, assumes a different dimension when performed by the celebrity. Ordinary acts such as road accidents, extra-marital affairs, alcoholism or financial mismanagement become transgressions when a celebrity is involved. *It moves from being a mere misdemeanour to being a transgression.*

Here the *scale* or *magnitude* of the event or action is what makes the celebrity, as Anna Kurian suggests (2008, Personal Communication). Thus a one-off killing (as in any murder) does not make the killer a celebrity, nor does a bomb. However, if the act involves serial killings or spectacular bombings (9/11 is a case in point) then we have celebrities. Thus celebrity culture is not only about excesses of lifestyle but also excessive use or deployment of other things, such as excessive violence, coercion, villainous corruption (the multi-million Telgi stamp paper scam is an instance) and so on.

The culture of celebrity has ensured that confessions and revelations are now conventional in celebrity write-ups, interviews and biographies. That is, admitting to substance abuse, marital problems and depression is a part of the aura of the celebrity itself. In fact, the celebrity has to have a transgressive aspect because it sets her or him apart as a singular individual, one who operates according to a different set of rules and norms.

The Structure of Scandal

The hero gone all wrong.
> On Mohammad Azharuddin and the match-fixing scandal.
> — Headline on rediff.com[2]

Hyderabad MLA caught in traffic (king) jam.
> On human trafficking scandal.
> — Headline on ibnlive.com[3]

What constitutes a scandal? And what form does scandal take in the mass media? Celebrity ecology utilises scandal as a prop for the celebrity's iconic status precisely by probing the limits of acceptability of celebrity behaviour and social or cultural tolerance. Scandals enable a questioning of the moral values of a culture. They are *dramas* that call into question our codes of conduct and norms about sexuality, duties, patriotism, efficiency and public life. They generate topics of conversation around issues of values, ethics, beliefs, responsibilities and the social structure. In a sense, a scandal, especially if it involves a man or woman in power (the allegations around Pratibha Patil in the run-up to the Indian Presidential elections, July 2007, is a case in point) *creates a culture of dialogue and discussion in the public sphere.* All prominent newspapers carried letters to the editor in the above debate.

A celebrity's individual experience or actions can mark the point of departure for larger debates about social issues and norms. The Clinton-Lewinsky case, which generated debates about a president's sexuality, and the possible exploitation of female employees in high office, and the more recent Paul

Wolfowitz case (2007) where the debates centred on the misuse of power for personal gain and favouritism, are a few examples. Thus scandals are not only about entertainment and titillation, they also serve another purpose—debate in the public sphere. Although it could be argued that personal scandals often hog the media limelight at the cost of more serious public issues like health or welfare, scandals often become the means of larger debates and even court intervention. The court ruling in the scandal and subsequent investigation of the Jessica Lall murder case is an example of how public outrage at the sordid scandal and even more sordid, clearly biased investigation energised a section of the legal community into acting.[4]

The Story, Other than the News

Paris Hilton arrested on DUI suspicion.

— Headline on CNN.com[5]

Though Indian stars may make charges of abuse and infidelity, it would be hard to find the lurid details plastered across newspapers and over the Internet...

— Comment, 19 December 2006 (David 2006)

A scandal, especially those involving celebrities, is usually cast as a story rather than as news.[6] It might begin as a news item, but the extended reportage on the news item makes it a media *scandal*. The story of Bill Clinton and Monica Lewinsky, of affairs between film stars and fraudulent transactions of politicians are constructed less as news items than as sensational stories.

'Gossip', writes Roger Wilkes in his study of scandals (2002), 'has specific raw ingredients: scandal, rumour, glamour and scurrility'. 'The best gossip', he goes on to add, 'consists of a mixture of sex, disclosure and a distinct whiff of danger' (Wilkes 2002: 3). Ruth David's complaint about the lack of 'juicy details' in her article on Bollywood divorces (cited at the head of this section) must be located in this context and structure of scandal: no lurid details implies that the scandal is not fascinating enough.

The audience obtains a certain amount of pleasure from the story. Elizabeth Bird suggests that a 'scandal story' evokes a pleasure derived from both the fascination with and revulsion for the social mess that scandals symptomatise (Bird 2003: 45). It is also a matter of interest to the readers as to what is *left out* of the news stories. It is this kind of indiscretion, failings, follies and deviance that the main news story leaves out that fuels gossip and scandal (Wilkes 2002: 5). We are both attracted to the transgression or impropriety committed and repulsed by it, and the story builds on this same paradox. Thus, when *Society* magazine carried a piece on the alleged extra-marital affair of prominent socialite Queenie Dhody (May 2007), letters to the editor in the subsequent issue expressed both outrage and fascination. One declared in a tone of high moral rectitude that she did not want to read a magazine that had 'stooped so low to carry a scandal', and would henceforth cancel her subscription. Another reader apparently did some fact-checking and declared that some of the facts reported were inaccurate.[7]

Gossip writing is often formulaic and sensationalist.[8] Attention-grabbing headlines characterise the genre: 'Is the Salman-Padma Marriage a Farce?' (*Society*, June 2007) and 'Shilpa's Lower Half is Sexier than Mine—Shamita Shetty' (*Moviemag*, July 2007). Photo features, interviews, news are genres common to all celebrity gossip writing. Celebrity marriage break-ups, new relationships, homes, feuds are common topics when it comes to themes in such writing.[9]

Gossip is essentially 'pop lore' (Zeitlin 1979). Gossip, especially about celebrities and integral to celebrity scandal takes the form of a 'difficult-to-believe-but-it-is-true' tone. This is further buttressed by providing evidence. Scandal relies on speculation. Hence, if we read the evidence closely we discover that we can no more trust the evidence than the subject or theme it is supposedly evidence of. Thus when we read a report that says: 'X was seen dining with Y in a restaurant' as incontrovertible *evidence* of the fact that 'X and Y have a relationship', neither the evidence nor the fact is more believable.

Gossip relies upon mixing positive and negative attributes of the celebrity in question. These attributes, such as physical beauty, intelligence, talent, are themselves *socially* ascribed and *valued as talents*. The positive-negative mix could be in various realms, though the one that seems to be most dominant is that of sexual morality. Thus physical beauty of Aishwarya Rai, Bipasha Basu, John Abraham is the positive quality that enables gossip about alleged negative ones such as promiscuity, marital discord or sexual infidelity. The 2006–2007 debate about the supposed Bipasha-John Abraham break-up often focussed on the wonderful couple the two goodlooking stars make.[10] Thus, their discord seems to be a negative development in a relationship between beautiful people.

Gossip also relies on the right mix of the factually correct and the questionable or doubtful. Thus we are aware that Bipasha Basu had commented on Saif Khan's sex appeal on *Koffee with Karan*, in John Abraham's presence. This is indisputable. Now look at the reconstruction of the same in this narrative:

> Now, now, don't get your knotty minds all into a tangle. It's just that *apni* gorgeous Bipasha Basu admitted on *Koffee with Karan* that she finds Saif Ali Khan *tres* hot, while John Abraham looked on nonchalantly. Well, it has come to pass that Bips and Saifoo bonded big time on the sets of *Race*. But that's that. There's nothing more to it. Some eyewitnesses aver that John Abraham was hitting the high spots in London sans Bips while shooting for *Goal*. Hmmm.[11]

The narrative shifts from a *rhetoric of fact* ('Bipasha Basu admitted on *Koffee with Karan* that she finds Saif Ali Khan *tres* hot') to a *rhetoric of uncertainty* (John Abraham's look as expressing nonchalance and the evidence of an unnamed eyewitness to his London behaviour). It is this crossing of the factual with the speculative and the questionable that constitutes gossip. The consequence, in the case of celebrity culture, is that such gossip and rumour enters the popular belief structure, and can never be fully removed from the biography of an individual. We cannot read about any celebrity, or their own autobiographies, for that matter, without being aware of these meta-textual (outside the actual text of the biography), elements (Cloete 2003).

Human Interest

Scandals figure as one kind of human interest story. Although scandals are invariably associated with sex, sleaze or corruption, they are dramatic, personal and therefore akin to stories of special individuals, heroism, catastrophe or drama. Scandals possess the same human appeal as the story of, say Budhia, the young marathon runner who seems to possess phenomenal energy or Sudha Chandran, the woman who lost her leg, acquired a Jaipur foot and went on to be a successful movie star.

Scandal narratives are essentially a *theatre of the dramatised real*. The dramatised real is constructed as a theatrical, exaggerated version of the real where some facts are mixed with partial falsehoods, plain speculation or, more importantly, with stereotypes that may or may not be relevant to this particular context or narrative. This dramatised real is *not* deliberately misleading or false, but rather conveys a *more dramatic version of events by drawing on probable contexts and sequence of events*. Headlines like 'Kangna and Her Italian Doctor'[12] or 'Saif Ali Khan Comes to Ex-girlfriend Rosa's Aid'[13] are meant to dramatise whatever is happening in celebrity lives. These dramatisations build on a reservoir of common knowledge and stereotypes. Traditional human-interest stories, for instance, focus on the bodily struggles of, say, Budhia or Lance Armstrong. These serve to heighten the human element of the celebrity or achievement by drawing attention to struggles that we *know* would be associated with sporting glory. Yet the narratives foreground these so that the real is rendered more dramatic for consumption.

Gossip and scandal thrives on the enhancement of follies to fit stereotypes. The celebrities are either good or bad, their actions either good or evil, with no scope for grey areas. It is this *magnification* of their acts, acts that we, the ordinary people, also do, for the purpose of shock that constitutes scandal.

Tabloid journalism thrives on the dramatised real of scandal. In reports about extra-marital affairs, for instance, the reportage also slips in a few sentences about quarrels between the individuals concerned. There is no reliable eye-witness account to such quarrels. However, the story relies on reader awareness that such quarrels and events are integral to fraught situations. Here the real is *dramatised* by appealing to our common, *a priori* knowledge and expectation of the *situation rather than factual accuracy*. It is in this shift from the real (the affair) to the dramatised real (the quarrels, the lachrymose situation, the elaborate rituals of leaving home or reconciliation) that scandals find their audience.

Sensational headlines and stories build on *our* fears, anxieties and desires. Indeed *scandals appeal because they deal with the moral values, fears or fantasies of the people as a whole* (Bird 2003: 32). Social values and norms are violated by scandals, and this is what interests us, that *individuals* are able to break social norms. Our anxieties about broken marriages or families, of being failures, our secret desires for wealth or fame (surely the story of a corrupt officer worth millions instils a vague sense of envy and admiration!) or our secret fantasies, especially in sexual encounters, fuel our reading of scandal. Tabloids thus require and feed an audience's fears and fantasies, in what is a circle of scandal consumption and production.

What is clear is that, in the case of scandals, it is not simply a media *production*. It is the sustained interest of the *audience* that generates greater media coverage. It could be argued that it was the high audience interest that *sustained* the extraordinary media coverage of the Clinton scandal.

We do not follow scandals for information. We follow them for their human aspect. What kind of information could we possibly derive from the Clinton case? Scandals seek to capture this human angle, even at the risk of sounding like speculation.

Film magazines are integral to the celebrity ecology and its scandal component. These start scandals by *hinting* at affairs and relationships of the rich and famous. Hence tabloids report that 'X was seen with Y at a restaurant' or that 'one ignored two at a party because two was apparently getting close to three recently'. Although the information is incomplete, the speculative process has been launched with such suggestions, and much celebrity talk revolves around speculation.

Speculation is central to scandal because it leaves the audience free to interpret the story in any which way they like. It invites us to speculate: 'Is X really seeing Y?' Keeping the story *open* without confirming or denying the news just reported is what enables such speculation.

One would recall the intense speculation about whether Abhishek would really marry Aishwarya Rai. Our interest in this wedding was fuelled by the fact that all we got was speculation, and all that was reported was hearsay and gossip. A definitive story would not call for speculation, and would therefore possess less dramatic elements. Speculation directly leads to drama, even melodrama, and therefore transforms the detail, rumour or story into a human interest story and a celebrity one.

Morality and Moral Panics

Shilpa Shetty and Richard Gere indulged in a shameless public display, it was not at all in keeping with our culture and tradition.

– Shiv Sena MP Sanjay Raut[14]

Child abuse and violence against children have emerged as one of the most crucial and alarming problems in the country.

– Report of the Committee investigating into Allegations of
Large Scale Sexual Abuse, Rape and Murder of
Children in Nithari Village of Noida.
(Ministry of Women and Child Development 2007)

Arguably the stories that most capture the audience interest are those that relate to morality, especially sexual morality.

Stories that blur boundaries of acceptable or unacceptable behaviour, that subvert what the particular culture or society has accepted as a moral code are the ones that constitute scandal. Scandals reveal to a society and culture the possibilities of their norms and values being subverted. They generate moral dilemmas, such as 'should we worry about our leaders' private lives as long as they function well in their offices and fulfil their responsibilities?'

What shocked and interested the near global audience about the Clinton scandal was that a celebrity figure could commit adultery and lie about it. The licentiousness of the president was seen as unacceptable because as the president he ought to have possessed greater moral values. Yet, as Douglas Kellner points out, many apolitical Americans were shocked more by the obnoxiousness of his prosecutors, such as Kenneth Starr, in pursuing the sexual escapade (Kellner 2003: 172). Likewise the Reverend Jesse Jackson scandal of early 2001. Reverend Jackson had had an illegitimate daughter from a former aide and he had been paying child maintenance in secret for some time. It was built on the fact that such a respected member of society could also indulge in such sordid acts of immorality.

At this point it might be necessary to point out the difference between a politician's sleaze or sex scandal and that of any other celebrity. In the Euro-American case, it has been argued that moral scandals around a politician is of a different order. Does the scandal, or are her or his sexual intrigues relevant to or prevent her or his political achievements or official work? Do we need to know what the politician's personal life is like? Yet the Clinton case revealed the other side to this question. Does not the sexual conduct and moral codes of a man occupying a public office become a matter of public interest? Does not the character of the man in public office—what can be called the 'character theme' in celebrity scandal—matter to the tax-payer (Bird 2003: 43–4)?

In India the politician's sex scandals receive far less media and public interest. The politician's morality, especially in the sexual arena, is of far less consequence than the morality in other professions. Indeed, one expects the politician to not have a morality! This is perhaps the reason why sex scandals involving film stars receive greater coverage.

However, morality is also linked to scandals that *acquire* celebrity status, and whose perpetrators or central characters achieve notoriety. The scandalisation of public life, a feature of every culture, often triggers larger debates that bestow the event(s) with a celebrity status. Social theorists have pointed to the existence of moral panics that occur whenever scandals or startling incidents such as paedophilia (surely the most significant moral panic of the twentieth century[15]), AIDS (Critcher 2003) or drug parties are reported. Celebrity scandals in India, such as the Pune rave party involving college students, the 2007 Orkut murders, the Jessica Lall murder case involving a celebrity model and a politician's son, or the cases involving Salman Khan and Sunjay Dutt, or Richard Gere-Shilpa Shetty, often kick-start debates about collapsing values, westernisation of Indian culture, the lax morals of the elite and the corruption of Indian youth. Counter arguments initiated by the celebrity scandal would include a defence of resilient Indian traditions, the question of authoritarianism, reassertion of faith in the judiciary and the question of adaptation.

Moral panics emerging from celebrity scandals often take on particular forms of narrative. First, there is a detailed analysis of the specific event itself. Second, the debate extends to a worry about how the problem can affect other areas and categories of people. Third, the debate centres on the nature of evil itself.[16]

The Pune rave party, resulting in the arrest of 270 youth, including students, a few foreign nationals and software engineers, in March 2007 sparked off a variety of debates that approximates to a moral panic. One response ran thus:

> At the heart of the present crisis of the urban youth lies the insufficiency of traditional models of ethics to govern lives of the young in contemporary India, prompted by late capitalism and a dominant consumer culture.[17]

Yet another opinion ran thus:

> It made one puke to learn that Pune city, once the seat of learning and erudition in Maharashtra, has now become a centre for 'rave parties' of the student community. Drugs on the soil made sacrosanct by the likes of Gopal Krishna Gokhale, Lokmanya Tilak and Veer Savarkar is what our youth has made of modernism born of globalisation. (Lavakare 2007)

Letters from readers expressed outrage. 'The youth should not waste their surplus income on things that ruin their health and our culture', wrote one.[18]

After the August 2007 fabricated sting operation to catch a teacher who allegedly pushed school girls into prostitution, debates shifted to moral codes for the media, again moving from the specific event to larger social and political questions.[19]

Here the narratives move from a specific event (present crisis) to the location of a source of evil. The hierarchy is very clear: from the lower rung of a present crisis to a greater problem such as the perceived absence of ethics and western consumer-capitalism.

A counter argument was forwarded by the editorial in *The Times of India*, which described the police who made the arrests as 'party poopers':

> What the morality-mongers want to do, however, is to narrow the space for celebration as much as possible. It's they who ought to be considered un-Indian, rather than anybody else. When enough serious crimes take place across the country we don't really need a replica of Taliban's moral police—it's a cop-out to reduce policing to hanging out undercover at bars and parties in an attempt to safeguard public morality.[20]

From another context Cho Sueng Hui, the Virginia Tech killer (2007) became an example of an immigrant who could not adapt to American culture. He also becomes emblematic of a social condition of immigrants and a social problem of maladjustment. Detailed reports and stories about the individual's violent actions and death often become starting points for debates about gun control in the USA, the racial problem, the immigrant problem and the American education system. Soon after the shooting, NDTV reported the revival of the gun control debate (Jacob 2007).[21] It triggers a moral panic.[22]

In the case of the writings on the Pune rave party scandal, the source of the panic's emergence or origin is a condition—westernisation and consumerism. The media, as Chas Critcher's work on moral panics has pointed out (2003), plays a significant role in constructing images of panics and crises and identifying causes. Expectedly, the Indian media played up the stereotypes of moneyed but unthinking youth, as seen in the first two opinions quoted above. The media hypes the crisis in its coverage, treating the event as a symbol of the collapse of Indian culture as a whole. A fair amount of distortion and exaggeration goes into the reportage. At this point, what Chas Critcher following Stan Cohen's 1973 model, calls moral entrepreneurs step in (Critcher 2003: 152). Commentators such as the ones cited above immediately offer explanations, stake claims to represent the victims or perpetrators and in general enable propaganda.

Questions of cultural limitations, moral policing, authoritarianism, legal measures and possible solutions result from such media attention. Richard Gere was served a court notice, the Jessica Lall case was re-opened and in both cases media representations and moral entrepreneurs were the cause. In the Gere-Shetty, case moral entrepreneurs worked the 'insult-to-Indian-culture' angle. In the second, the question of public life, its morality and power over the legal system was the centre of attention. Moral panics clearly have some long-term effects when legislation and other state measures are put in place due to the pressure in civil society. Scandals such as the Pune rave party or the Jessica Lall case are celebrity scandals because they have a role beyond the immediate context: they acquire high visibility for being iconic. They are *celebrity* scandals because they supposedly represent a greater crisis of a culture. Just as celebrities represent a collective social-cultural fantasy and index of success with commercial, cultural and political edges, celebrity scandals triggering moral panics represent cultural anxieties.

Humanising Celebrity

One way of looking at celebrity misbehaviour or faults is to see them as collapsing the distinction between ordinary or extraordinary that separates us from the stars. Messy marriages, financial bungling, substance abuse, and other such mistakes humanise celebrities, bring them down to earth, as it were. Maybe, as Roger Wilkes puts it, 'gossip about the unhappy lives of the stars helps us contend with our own ordinariness' (Wilkes 2002: 323). In order to understand this better we can situate celebrity scandals within the structure of selfhood and identity in the contemporary age.

Celebrity culture's ecology via mass media representation constructs the star as somebody above the average human. Stars are those bestowed with talents, looks and powers that the regular human lacks. In addition, they have been able to utilise these talents, looks and power to the fullest extent possible. Their success, financial and cultural, is an index of this utilisation. Thus we can see the celebrity as somebody who has *transcended* the usual problems of everyday life and other humans to become successful.

This theme of transcendence is played out in almost every celebrity interview. The interview or biography of the celebrity is an exercise in the construction of an identity, of a self. This self is one that has overcome major obstacles to become successful. Rakhi Sawant in her conversation on *Koffee with Karan* underscores her middle class origins, her efforts to care for the family after their father abandoned them and her struggles in the film industry. The image she projects is of a person who has become a star only by dint of her determination, talent and personal effort. A similar celebrity is Mallika Sherawat.

At the age of 21 she was on the cover of the Indian edition of *Cosmopolitan*. Stories of her background, her conservative family and her determination to make it as a star in an industry where connections and lineage decide futures have circulated since her controversial debut, *Khwahish*.²³

This is image-making that sets the celebrity above the ordinary individual, and is a key component of celebrity culture. Where others would have caved-in in the face of difficulties, Rakhi Sawant toiled on and became a celebrity.

One argument made about our continued fascination with celebrities is that they represent a fantasy, a perfection that we, ordinary people cannot hope to attain: of looks, money, power, visibility and success. They are, in this argument, fantasy objects, and 'hold out the lure of a fully-achieved selfhood' to those who yearn for such an impossible fullness and perfection (Gilbert 2004: 91).

This argument helps us understand the interest in celebrity dysfunction or transgressions. It also helps us locate the essential paradox of celebrity culture. On the one hand the media focuses on the perfection, appeal, success and value of the celebrity. On the other, this same media reveals the tragedies, imperfections and unacceptable aspects of the same celebrity.

Although it is easy to see celebrity culture as actively encouraging, constructing and disseminating the cult of perfection, meritocracy and success by producing fantasy objects like beautiful models, successful film stars and sportsmen and women worth millions, we must also recognise it as a culture that humanises them. Celebrity culture is caught in the *paradox of deification that renders them perfect and godly, and humanisation that makes them more human*. Scandals and transgressions are highlighted, reported and relished as a means of debunking the myth of human perfection, and is intrinsic to celebrity culture. One mode of humanising celebrities is to focus on their ailments, ranging from the physical to the psychological.²⁴

On 20 January 2005, one of Bollywood's popular heroines of the 1970s and 1980s, Parveen Babi, died mysteriously, and triggered a spate of writings about her mental state. Parveen Babi had starred in hugely successful movies like *Deewar* (1975), *Amar Akbar Anthony* (1977), *Shaan* (1980) and *Namak Halaal* (1982). Her co-stars have included mega-stars like Amitabh Bachchan. She graced the cover of *Time* in 1977, one of the biggest recognitions of her career in which she more often than not portrayed the unconventional Indian woman. For a considerable period of time she lived in New York, returning to Mumbai in 2002, and immediately embroiling herself in controversies. She accused several former co-stars, including Amitabh Bachchan, of conspiring to murder her. She claimed she had evidence relating to the 1993 Mumbai blasts, but, when summoned by the court, did not turn up, expressing fears of being killed. She became a recluse, and, having put on considerable weight became unrecognisable as the former beauty. She returned to visibility indirectly with *Woh Lamhe* (2006), which was supposedly based on her life. Mahesh Bhatt, who made *Woh Lamhe* had earlier made (*Arth*, 1982), again a film based on his relationship with Babi. The Wikipedia found her life and death interesting enough to post an entry, and claimed she might have been schizophrenic.[25] 123India.com reiterated this claim in an undated news item:

> Perhaps the root cause of her exit from stardom to the confinement of an apartment was the genetically acquired mental ailment 'schizophrenia', a disease that unlike others arouses not sympathy but disdain for the victim in our society...Day after day followed and Parveen Babi struck [sic] to her self imposed confinement. Only an occasional spewing of venom against some co-stars broke her silence. But no one took her seriously. Everybody knew that she was mentally off balance.[26]

The Times of India commented:

> Her close friends admitted privately that the actress, a post-graduate in psychology, had turned an emotional wreck. (Mishra 2005)

The Telegraph writing on 23 January 2005, soon after her death, described her has having led a 'tragically lonely life in the failed quest for love'.[27] Chandrima Bhattacharya writing in *The Telegraph* also claimed that she had schizophrenia, and quoted Vinod Khanna as speculating on Babi's mental problem (Bhattacharya 2005). Amitabh Bachchan who made films with Parveen Babi than with any other star, except Jaya Bhaduri, commented to Subhash K. Jha for rediff.com:

> It wouldn't be ethical to talk about her condition. The nature of her illness was such that she was terrified of people; she wanted to be left alone. She deliberately distanced herself from everyone. (Jha 2005)

Most commentators also made it a point to mention that Babi was an unconventional heroine. Amitabh Bachchan said of her, '[she] brought in a new, bohemian kind of leading lady to the screen' (Jha 2005). *The Telegraph* piece described her thus: 'the ultimate epitome of Bollywood's Bohemian rhapsody'.[28] For the *Times of India* she was 'the symbol of the "New" woman'.[29] The references to her Bohemian style and the unusual roles add up to construct the image of an unconventional star. The fact that she starred in so many commercially successful films, and opposite the biggest star of the industry, Amitabh Bachchan, aligned with the aspect of her Bohemian life implicitly links madness with disordered life, success and fame.[30] And *Woh Lamhe*, of course, explicitly linked madness with celebrity status in the character of Kangna Ranaut.

Such representations of the madness of a celebrity dramatise the self-destructive elements even in apparently successful people. It humanises them when we read of the hugely successful Parveen Babi being described as an emotional wreck or as an insecure person afraid of the sound of the doorbell. Yet these representations of humanised celebrity also serve another purpose, a purpose that enhances the celebrity-hood of the tortured, anxiety-ridden star.

The stereotype of the mad genius as seen in films about celebrities like Sylvia Plath or Howard Hughes, and, in India, in representations of the allegedly schizophrenic Parveen Babi, the alcoholic Rajesh Khanna, or the prior drug addiction of Sunjay Dutt promotes a certain self-identity. Sunjay Dutt has openly spoken of his drug addiction. We now have Lindsay Lohan and Paris Hilton who admit to needing rehabilitation programmes and psychiatric help for substance abuse. Such admissions suggest a self-identity, driven, in a great part, by the media and publicity machinery of the stars, which is *artistic*. We do not hear so much about sport stars who are similar sufferers, do we? In the case of literary figures, biographies and commentaries thrive on the madness, obsessions and eccentricities of these tortured geniuses. Contemporary examples from the twentieth century would include celebrity authors Sylvia Plath, Anne Sexton, Ernest Hemingway, Robert Lowell, T.S. Eliot, Ezra Pound, Antonin Artaud in each case connecting of this madness with creativity and fame. A biography of Plath, by Anne Stevenson, is thus leadingly titled *Bitter Fame*.[31]

There is an intrinsic connection suggested between their creative professions, acting, writing, inventing, and their madness or disturbed minds. The narratives of the dramatised real in the case of these writers, actors and artists builds on the stereotype of the mad genius. Mental problems, whether depression or manic symptoms, resulting from substance abuse or stressful lives in the limelight somehow become a part of their identity. In some cases, such as Dutt's, the star's subsequent success is therefore *part of an identity that suggests a heroic triumph over medical-pathological odds*. In the case of Parveen Babi, and this calls for a *gendered* reading of mental illness and celebrity culture, it ends with tragedy. We must note that films made about such mad writers, *The Hours* about Woolf and *Sylvia* about Plath, both end with the death of the woman protagonist. Surely a significant point?

Thus mental illness and/or disorder is linked to film celebrity culture as a near-romanticised state of the madness of creative life—an old theme, from the madness of Greek poets to Van Gogh. Mental disorder renders their celebrity status more interesting and worthwhile: a life that purchases creative success at great cost to the mind.

It thus serves two purposes: it renders the celebrity more human, while setting her or him apart from us as somebody whose artistic creativity generates disorder. She or he triumphs despite the disorder. The aura of the celebrity is enhanced, I suggest, through the scandal of madness or substance abuse. And so the paradox of celebrity culture persists:

1. The successful Parveen Babi, isolated by her madness, seems just *one of us*;
2. And yet her successful career, perhaps battling such emotional trauma while portraying unconventional (bohemian) roles, projects a determined, talented *artist, unique* and *distinct* from ordinary people.

The theme of risk here is of being a part of an industry where true relationships are not possible and where one is frequently lonely. The coverage of Parveen Babi's death mentioned this aspect of Bollywood. Thus the discussion of celebrity mental illness somehow swerves into comments about the hazards of the career and the insensitivity of the profession itself.

Related to this theme of celebrity and mental illness is the theme of celebrity illness. Cycling champion Lance Armstrong repute is not merely due to his phenomenal successes on the track but partly due to the well-known facts of his battle with and triumph over cancer. From Amitabh Bachchan's injury during the making of *Coolie*, Saif Ali Khan's recent heart problems, Christopher Reeves in a wheel-chair, stories of SRK's back problems, Leander Paes' brain disease, and Sachin Tendulkar's fitness worries are aligned on the same plane as scandals and celebrity mistakes because of what I have called *strategies of the dramatised real*, as scandals and celebrity mistakes. For people who have overwhelmed odds and obstacles, such mishaps are humanising dimensions, especially when their pain and suffering of the dramatised real become central to the narrative. Periodically we receive news of a particular actor being injured during filming. Celebrity injuries and illnesses have attracted considerable attention, and details of the nature of their illness, the treatment, the recovery have all been part of the publicity machinery. The most famous of such cases in the 1980s was Sudha Chandran, who despite a false leg, continued a career in dance. *Mayuri* (1986), the film based on her life, and starring Chandran herself, became a runaway success and catapulted her into superstardom. The film was given a tax-exemption and was promoted as an inspirational tale of a woman's battle against injury and failure. It made her career.

Stephen Harper looking at madness and celebrity culture argues that representations of mental problems among stars serves to *highlight* the risk involved in being famous (Harper 2006: 325).[32] This argument could be applied to celebrity injuries and disease as well. Many of the reports detailing injuries locate the injury in the working life of the individual. The most famous recent case is SRK's back. It is common knowledge that he overworks, and the injured back seems to be the price he pays. Indeed, SRK has admitted in his interviews that surgery is the price he must pay for his success (Khan 2003). Such revelations underline the risk culture that dovetails into celebrity culture. The ending of the hugely successful Clint Eastwood film *Million Dollar Baby* (2004) underscores this aspect. Hillary Swank lying paralysed in hospital from an injury suffered in the boxing ring, wants to be taken off the life support systems: having stood up to hear the cheers of the audience, she cannot bear to be lying helpless any more. Her injury is the price she must pay for the glory.

However, to go back to the questions we began with, why should celebrity disease attract so much attention? In her study of women magazine readers, cultural critic Joke Hermes reported many readers admitting that 'the misery of others made them feel better about their own lives' (Hermes 1999: 80). Hermes goes on to suggest that such reports create a 'repertoire of melodrama' to which the audience relates (Hermes 1999: 80). This could be one way of understanding the reasons for extensive coverage of celebrity illness and injury.

The humanising of celebrities corresponds to what Graeme Turner has called the 'demotic turn' in celebrity culture (Turner

2004: 82–6). Due to this demotic turn more ordinary people get the chance via contests, talent searches, Reality Television to become celebrities. The demotic turn also means that celebrities are increasingly less God-like. Hence media representations of these stars often seek reality in their lives leading to the coverage of their mental problems, illnesses and injuries.

Celebrity and Damage

You have vandalized my heart, raped my soul and torched my conscience. You thought it was one pathetic boy's life you were extinguishing. Thanks to you, I die like Jesus Christ, to inspire generations of the weak and the defenceless people.
> — Cho Sueng Hui, Virginia Tech killer in his videotape.[33]

'Koli Did It: CBI' screams the headlines from *The Tribune* (23 March 2007), quoting the CBI charge sheet that blamed Pandher's servant, Surinder/Subhash Koli for the grisly Nithari murders. As of 11 July 2007, 8 charge sheets have been filed, all against Koli, charging him with rape and murder.

The Oklahoma City bomber and the Unabomber, our own Charles Shobraj and Phoolan Devi, Babubhai Katara and 'D' [Dawood Ibrahim]... the list of people who have become celebrities through their acts of outrage is extensive. But why and how does a gruesome act acquire celebrity status?

What I call *celebrity damage* refers both to damage that *leads* to celebrity status for the perpetrator, such as Moninder Singh Pandher-Surinder Koli and the Nithari killings, Dawood Ibrahim and the Mumbai blasts, Katara and human trafficking, and the damage suffered *by* celebrities. The word fame originally meant good reputation. Evidently, this would mean that serial killers, criminals and crooks would not be famous in the true sense of the word. Lee Harvey Oswald who shot John F Kennedy, Nathuram Godse who killed Mahatma Gandhi, John Wilkes Booth who assassinated Abraham Lincoln have retained their visibility just a shade below that of their famous victims. Thus in the age of mass media and technologies of hyper-visibility, the line between fame and notoriety is frequently blurred.

Celebrity culture today arguably thrives less on merit or talent than on visibility. And crooks, killers and criminals find the same degree of visibility, at least for a short duration, as the others. Leo Braudy, in one of the first studies of fame and celebrity culture, argues that fame became associated with *visibility* in twentieth-century USA. And once fame is marked by visibility rather than achievement, notoriety is just as good. Leo Braudy puts it best:

> Fame promises acceptability, even if one commits the most heinous crime, because thereby people will finally know who you are, and you will be saved from the living death of being unknown. (Braudy 1986: 562)

As in the endurance and trauma-inducing performances of illusionists, magicians and sports stars, assassins, terrorists and criminals acquire high visibility through their performances. Since celebrity today is to do less with merit or positive achievements, we could suggest that fame and notoriety are on the same continuum or plane.

Celebrity damage is not merely about celebrities like Salman Khan, accused of illegal or anti-social acts, but about serial killers and criminals who acquire notoriety when the media generates widespread interest in their actions.[34]

Indeed it could be argued that individuals are able to acquire widespread fame through their performances *because* the mass media facilitates this. Assassins and criminals send messages and information to the mass media. Thus Cho Sueng Hui, the 2007 Virginia Tech killer, sent his homemade tape showing him armed and angry to television stations. Many, like Phoolan Devi, become the subject of famous films or biographies.

The mass media erodes the distinction between good and bad performances, rendering both equally visible, even though moral judgements and descriptions may encode the news items and stories. The organising principle of the news about killers or terrorists is about the *individuals*. In this there is little to distinguish between the coverage of Mohammed Yusuf, the Nobel Laureate and cooperative micro-finance wizard from Bangladesh, and Surinder Koli or Cho Sueng Hui. The individuals are the subjects of news reports, public debates and professional opinions. This is often achieved by *transforming the criminal into an emblematic figure of what is wrong with our culture*—a moral crisis or panic. Take the case of Cho Sueng Hui, the latest to acquire such notoriety. Even Indian newspapers carried visuals of the killer. The coverage included opinions on what had gone wrong with this immigrant to the land of plenty. Also central to celebrity damage, especially the celebrification of serial killers, is the way performance and identity fuse. In the case of Surinder Koli, Manu Sharma, Phoolan Devi or M.S. Pandher, *they are famous for being themselves*. The serial killer or mass murderer is not playing a role or putting on a performance that attracts attention—he is simply being and playing *himself*. This natural state attracts attention. We are interested in their habits, lifestyle, childhood, and very often the media does ferret out information, the surfeit of details about the Glasgow airport bombers, their families, parents and early life is a case in point, because there is an unconscious subtext created for their celebrated life. This subtext suggests a link between what they are (damaged or sick) and what they do (maim or kill).

Celebrity damage and the attendant scandal depend also on the nature of the victims. Children-as-victims are the most consistent images in media reports of scandals. The construction of the innocent child, as studies have demon-strated (Jewkes 2004: 94–8),[35] enables the construction of the crime as *morally* monstrous and evil. The scandal drives a moral panic through this binary of innocent child versus monstrous stranger. Incidentally, it is the paedophilic *stranger* rather than the paedophile *within the family* who is the subject of attention in a moral panic.

Why does violence and violent death fascinate us, and why does its perpetrator become a celebrity? A media representation of violent death is now an ubiquitous phenomenon, even though excessive representations of war, famine or disease run the risk of inducing compassion fatigue (Moeller 1999). What celebrity damage does is, according to David Schmid, fulfill two requirements of modern life, the need for representation of death and the need for celebrities (Schmid 2006: 303). The serial killer, the mass murderer, the terrorist fulfil these two demands. The need for violent representations of death stems from an anxiety about it, where the images consumed in carefully controlled settings alleviate the anxiety.

The appeal of the criminal, according to critics, is that she or he appears heroic, at least to some of us. 'The narrative of the heroic criminal,' writes Paul Kooistra, 'helps us to vicariously release rebellious feelings generated by the restrictions imposed by authority' (Kooistra 1989: 10, 21). Walter Benjamin writing on violence also, likewise, notes 'how often the figure of "great" criminal, however, repellent his ends may have been, has aroused the secret admiration of the public' (Benjamin 1921[2002]). Films like *Ocean's 11, 12* and *13* showcase the spectacle of the clever criminal. In Hindi cinema, the anti-hero and the hero who transgresses the law or frequently becomes the 'Robin Hood' to serve the cause of social justice is an old theme. Amitabh Bachchan's roles in numerous films portrayed the rebel hero with a cause. Although the rebel hero was not truly a criminal, he definitely took the law into his own hands to serve a greater, just cause. The hero as trickster often hoodwinked the villain through con jobs or deceit, and the audience cheered. Such representations of the hero's actions as pardonable, appeal, according to this argument, to the larger desire to rebel against authority. Recent films like *Apna Sapna Money Money* (2006), *Golmaal* (2006) and *Bluffmaster* (2005) also focus on the abilities of a con artist to get rich and famous through illegitimate means. The criminal fits into this *culture of potential and desirable rebellion*, as a heroic figure who broke the law (though Kooistra excludes serial killers from this category of heroic criminals), or who made it good against all odds. Con artists who manage to fool the government or big business houses, hackers and such white collar criminals, such as Harshad Mehta, Rajan Pillai, Telgi, do possess an appeal for the cleverness with which they pulled off their heists. They become celebrities for this aspect, even if we do not necessarily support criminal actions.

As for mass murderers or serial killers, there is extensive media coverage of the murderer's house, lifestyle and habits. (Recall here the coverage of Pandher's house and his family and Cho Sueng Hui's lonely life.) The cult of the serial killer often takes recourse to such murderabilia, where the newspaper reader or consumer is offered insights into the life of the killer.[36] Indeed, regular murderers, who might kill their spouse, neighbour or somebody else, rarely attain celebrity status. It requires serial killings, something on a greater macabre scale, such as Pandher-Koli's work, to become celebrity news. Moninder Singh Pandher now has a Wikipedia entry (*http://en.wikipedia.org/wiki/Moninder_Singh_Pandher*). These become, in David Schmid's apposite phrase, 'idols of destruction', popular and notorious due to their destructiveness (Schmid 2006). Indeed, the serial killer and the mass murderer has, at least in American culture, attained cult status (Grixti 1995).

Many serial killers and mass murderers are driven by the need to get acclaim. They inform the police, write to the media, and even produce work from prison so that they can tell their story to the world. One example is the Oklahoma City bomber, Timothy McVeigh, whose actions claimed 168 lives in 1995. A Gulf War veteran, 33-year-old McVeigh, was finally executed in 2001. McVeigh gave interviews for a book (*American Terrorist* by Lou Michel and Dan Herbeck, HarperCollins, 2001) and figured thrice on *Time* magazine's cover (issues dated 1 May 1995, 16 June 1997, 21 May 2001). *Time* also interviewed him just before he went on trial. In this interview McVeigh complained that he had been demonised by the press. David Copeland, whose bombs killed three people in London (1999), and who was popularly known as the 'Soho Nail Bomber', claimed he wanted to get caught. He published a letter in *The Mirror* where, like McVeigh, he claimed he was misrepresented as a monster. *The Mirror* also published several extracts from his private letters, where he enquires about website and other media reports on him. As Chris Rojek has argued, Copeland was clearly making an attempt to acquire fame (Rojek 2001: 144–6). Perhaps the most famous case is that of Jack Henry Abbott. A convicted murderer, Abbott wrote long letters to novelist Norman Mailer, discussing prison life and violence. Mailer wrote a *New York Review of Books* article based on these letters and accompanied by notes by Abbott himself in a separate piece (Mailer 1981). The result was a US$ 12,000 advance from Random House to Abbott to write a book. The parole board released Abbott and his book *In the Belly of the Beast* was eventually published, making a tidy profit for Abbott. The fact that Norman Mailer pleaded his case made Abbott a literary celebrity. Closer to home, Charles Shobhraj, wrote the *Nepali Times*, had become something of a celebrity, despite being convicted for murder.[37] Described as a 'cultured, cunning, satanically handsome villain with a compulsion to do evil' in another article in this same issue (McBeth 2004), Shobhraj's anti-hero status is apparent in writings about his criminal career.

Thus one route to celebrity status is through damage, acts of violence and socially unacceptable acts. Chris Rojek argues that one reason for such routes to celebrity is due to the very nature of celebrity culture itself. 'There exists', Rojek suggests, 'a contradiction between the desire to achieve celebrity and the limited means of goal attainment'. Individuals therefore resort to illegitimate means to acquire fame. This is a convincing argument. Newspapers frequently carry reports of college-going youth who steal cell phones and motorcycles in order to support a lavish lifestyle.[38] An ATM guard in Hyderabad conned customers of their credit cards and made extravagant purchases on them, all because of his 'habituation to a luxurious lifestyle' which could not be supported by his 'meagre salary'.[39] The guard became a 15-second celetoid for his actions. These lifestyles that they wish to acquire and imitate are made available to them through the mass media's reports of celebrity lives. Although their jobs and salaries do not allow them to acquire the desired objects and lifestyles, crime begins to be an alternative. In a sense, then, this line of argument locates celebrity scandal and celebrity damage as the consequence of social inequalities and their psychological effects. Rojek proposes that 'democracy offers each individual the chance of social ascent, but part of the psychological allure of celebrity... resides in the gap between the theory and practice of democracy' (Rojek 2001: 178). That is, even though democracy theoretically offers the chance of individual advancement, actually existing conditions may not help this. The turn to illegitimate actions could be seen as rooted in this paradox. The emphasis on con artists and clever deals in the recent Hindi films mentioned above might mark this paradox.

However, celebrity damage need not be about killings, illegitimate or demonic actions that generate cult status for the perpetrator. Celebrity damage is also what is suffered *by* the celebrity as a result of inappropriate behaviour. SRK has, for instance, faced criticism for dancing at weddings for a fee. More recently, his bungalow at Bandra has attracted litigation.[40] Aamir Khan advertising for Coca Cola after scientific reports about pesticides in the drink also attracted opprobrium. In Chennai college students, mostly members of the organisation, Youth for Social Change, rallied with placards protesting Aamir Khan's support of the controversial soft drink.[41]

In a recent article that captures this de-auratisation of the celebrity Prashant Rane describes how film stars fall from pedestals because of their behaviour. Stars dance at weddings and behave badly on tours, running up huge telephone and laundry bills for themselves and their entourage. Actresses like Urmila 'charge to even attend a wedding and cosy up to the bride as if she were her best friend—all for a price'. What has knocked stars off their pedestal is their availability for any ridiculous event, from weddings to anniversaries to opening shops and so on.[42] Fame damage comes from the inability to understand one's celebrity status, the constant surveillance and the lack of fit between a natural tendency and one's expected role. It is for this reason that advice columns on how to behave at upscale parties are common in magazines and periodicals today (*Society*, May 2007).

Narratives about celebrity marriages and extra-marital affairs, the staple of scandal everywhere, is driven by the desire to know more about sexual and moral transgressions by stars. Even divorce lawyers who are often privy to celebrity marital scandals become celebrities themselves. Thus *Society* magazine carried a piece on Mridula Kadam, a family lawyer who 'has been privy to the private moments of innumerable celebrities whose marriages have broken down' (Bhatnagar 2007: 111–5). *Moviemag* takes great pleasure in hinting that famous director Aditya Chopra's equally famous father, Yash Chopra is livid because 'Adi is Not Divorced from First Wife Payal' but has 'tabloids aflame with his secret engagement to Rani Mukherjee'.[43]

Condemnation, resentment and sometimes even approval are the common responses to celebrity damage. Yet, I believe, it does not necessarily diminish the star's star value. What it does is to add something more to the celebrity. What it adds is a dose of slightly whimsical or even indelicate feature to the aura. We know that SRK does not need to dance at weddings in order to make money. We know that the top film and sports stars earn enough from their professions, and can afford to pay their telephone and laundry bills. When their greed or miserliness is revealed, what is added is a small taint, a slight flaw as is often deliberately introduced in works of art. I propose that the taint furnishes an additive to the celebrity. We are fascinated by the celebrity's pranks and indelicate behaviour even as we squirm at the thought that SRK needs to dance at weddings like any common minstrel or performer.

When the ordinary person on the street is filmed in a humorous or tragic situation (the candid camera genre on TV), we again have celebrity damage and celebrity scandal. MTV *Bakra* and now the *Baap of Bakra*, hosted by the irrepressible

Cyrus Broacha now a celebrity himself, inaugurated this and inspired a host of programmes on regional channels.[44] The woman or man on the street, going about her or his business becomes the subject of a practical joke. The 15 seconds of fame on nation wide television is primarily built on embarrassment resulting from being trapped in the joke—a scandal, etymologically, is a trap into which one falls!—and becoming the object of laughter. This is the newest kind of celebrity damage.

For sports stars, scandals range from bad performance (Sachin's poor form was a national shame) to substance abuse (Diego Maradona's being the most famous and Andrew Flintoff's drinking binges), drug-taking for enhanced performance (Shoaib Akhtar), sleaze and/or violence (Shane Warne, Mike Tyson) among others. Cheating, match-fixing, and corruption, charges dog cricket captains (Mike Atherton, of England, for example, Hansie Cronje and the South African team, Mohammed Azharuddin from India), on a regular basis now. In contemporary sports, the heroic deeds of the sports star are also suspect, with doubts about steroid intake and corruption. The celebrity body's fitness is not emulatable because it is often at the centre of the scandal. Where sports were once seen as unmediated and undiluted achievement, there prevails a great degree of ambiguity and suspicion about performance today.

So scandal thrives. Our sustained interest in what celebrities do and what they ought to do has created a roaring industry in tabloid culture.

Notes

1. 271 youngsters were caught at a Pune rave party in March 2007. For a news report see http://www.zeenews.com/znnew/articles.asp?aid=358061&sid=REG&ssid. 15 September 2007.
2. http://www.rediff.com/cricket/2000/nov/20azhar.htm (downloaded on 15 September 2007).
3. http://www.ibnlive.com/news/india/04_2007/ (downloaded on 15 September 2007).

4. Lall, a celebrity model, was shot dead in a prominent bar where she worked as a barmaid. The main accused, Manu Sharma, son of a leading Congress Party politician was acquitted in 2006 after a 7-year (bungled) investigation and court proceedings (which included testimonies by Malini Ramani (the owner of the bar and a celebrity socialite in Delhi). The ensuing public outcry and media coverage caused the higher court to re-open the case. Manu Sharma was eventually found guilty and sentenced to life imprisonment in December 2006.

5. http://www.cnn.com/2006/SHOWBIZ/TV/09/07/parishilton/index.html (downloaded on 15 September 2007).

6. I am here working with Elizabeth Bird's reading of the narrative of the scandal (Bird 2003: 21–50).

7. See letters by Anahita Vakharia, Anjali Khimji and Jyoti Malhotra, *Society*, June 2007, pp. 11–12.

8. There is considerable difference between rumour and gossip. Gossip concerns the personal life of individuals, while rumours are usually about events. Further, while rumour is almost always unsubstantiated, gossip might be verified. Hence writing about celebrities is usually gossip.

9. Critics have however argued that celebrity gossip magazines that have a greater female readership constitute a device of empowerment for the women. Further, a sharing of such gossip generates an imagined community of belonging for the magazine's readers. See, for instance, Feasey (2006: 183).

10. The two finally had to make public appearances and statements about still being together. See, for instance, 'United We Stand: Bipasha Basu and John Abraham', *Daily News and Analysis*, 7 July 2006. Available online at http://www.dnaindia.com/reports (downloaded on 6 February 2008).

11. *Filmfare*, July 2007, p. 25.

12. *Filmfare*, 15 October 2007.

13. *Filmfare*, June 2007.

14. 'Protest over Shilpa-Gere Kiss Justified: Sena', *Daily News and Analysis*, 17 April 2007. Available online at http://www.dnaindia.com/report.asp?NewsID=1091336 (downloaded on 15 September 2007).

15. Phillip Jenkins (1992), cited in Yvonne Jewkes (2004: 94).

16. I adapt this model of the 'hierarchy of discourses' in moral panics from Astroff and Nyberg (1992).

17. 'Reflections on the Rave Party', Metro Plus, *The Hindu*, 28 March 2007. Available online at http://www.hindu.com/thehindu/mp/2007/03/28/stories/2007032800930300.htm (downloaded on 15 September 2007).

18. Letters to the Editor, *The Hindu*, 8 March 2007. Available online at http://www.hindu.com/2007/03/08/stories/2007030801961001. htm (downloaded on 15 September 2007).

19. For a collection of articles on media codes, law and morality following this incident, see *Daily News and Analysis*, 9 September 2007, p. 8. Available online at http://epaper.dnaindia.com/epapermain. aspx?queryed=20&eddate=9/9/2007 (downloaded on 15 September 2007).

20. 'Party-poopers', *The Times of India*, 7 March 2007. Available online at http://timesofindia.indiatimes.com/OPINION/Editorial/ TODAYS_EDITORIAL_Party-poopers/articleshow/1728936.cms (downloaded on 15 September 2007).

21. 'The Virginia Tech Tragedy and Gun Control', 26 April 2007. Available online at http://www.worldpress.org/Americas/2768.cfm (downloaded on 13 July 2007).

22. In the case of Cho Sueng Hui the poet and faculty member at Virginia Tech, Nikki Giovanni, stated that Hui's creative work upset many students in the creative writing course. The alleged writings, now perhaps iconic as the work of a deranged mind, included extremely violent plays like *Richard McBeef*.

23. See, for instance, interviews on Indiatimes.com (1 April 2004, available online at http://movies.indiatimes.com/articleshow/594985. cms [downloaded on 13 July 2007]), SeasonsIndia.com (undated, available online at http://www.seasonsindia.com/cinemascope/ specInterviewSea.jsp?intId=2 [downloaded on 13 July 2007]) and rediff.com (5 June 2003, available online at http://www.rediff.com/ movies/2003/jun/05mallika.htm [downloaded on 13 July 2007]).

24. Stephen Harper has shown how mental illness narratives are common in celebrity culture (2006).

25. http://en.wikipedia.org/wiki/Parveen_Babi (downloaded on 7 July 2007).

26. http://123india.santabanta.com/cinema.asp?pid=4960 (downloaded on 7 July 2007).

27. http://www.telegraphindia.com/1050123/asp/nation/story_ 4287764.asp (downloaded on 7 July 2007).

28. http://www.telegraphindia.com/1050123/asp/nation/story_ 4287764.asp (downloaded on 7 July 2007).

29. http://timesofindia.indiatimes.com/articleshow/998600.cms (downloaded on 7 July 2007).

30. There have been numerous recent Hollywood films that also link madness with genius, success and celebrity status: *A Beautiful Mind* (2001), *The Hours* (2002), *Sylvia* (2003), *The Aviator* (2004) look at the minds of the mathematician John Nash, the writer Virginia

Woolf, the poet Sylvia Plath and the inventor-innovator, Howard Hughes, respectively.

31. It is interesting to note that many of these celebrity poets wrote what is called 'confessional poetry', where they examined their selves with great rigour and poetic power. In an extended, and perhaps unpardonable sense, this genre from celebrity poets in their madness and personal tragedies are the poetic equivalent of confessional talk shows where individuals reveal their anxieties, fantasies and fears. For a literary-critical study of confessional poetry and celebrity culture see David Haven Blake (2001).

32. The most famously tragic case would of course be that of Diana, Princess of Wales, who died in a road accident when trying to escape newspaper reporters.

33. Dated 17 April 2007, available online at http://news.bbc.co.uk/2/hi/americas/6570369.stm (downloaded on 15 September 2007).

34. Studied in detail by Leyton (1986).

35. The Report of the Committee investigating into Allegations of Large Scale Sexual Abuse, Rape and Murder of Children in Nithari Village of Noida (U.P.), underscores the innocence and vulnerability of especially migrant and homeless children, children of construction workers (p. 11).

36. Schmid uses the term 'murderabilia' (2006: 296–7) to describe the 'selling' of murder. Serial Killer Central (*www.skcentral.com*) offers art works by convicted killers. Supernaught.com (*www.supernaught.com*) offers items from killers' houses: a brick from Jeffrey Dahmer's house, a greeting card at $ 1700, a bathhouse membership card, a magazine he had ordered at $ 195, a lock of Charles Manson's hair (Dahmer was found guilty of torturing—including mutilation, necrophilia, cannibalism—at least 17 people, some of them children, to death. He was beaten to death in prison in 1994, but not before he became the hero of a comic book biography published in Milwaukee in 1992. Charles Manson founded a cult in 1967 and was responsible for several murders). An index of the fascination with serial killers is the stupendous success—including 5 Academy Awards in 1992—of *The Silence of the Lambs* and the popularity of Hannibal Lecter as celefiction. It is crucial to see famous villains in myth, literature and history—Dracula, Frankenstein's monster, Ravana, Emperor Nero, Jack the Ripper, Adolf Hitler, Voldemort, Professor Moriarty—as part of a culture of celebrity villainy where deviance and criminality become the modes of fame-gathering. In this, we need to see fictional villains alongside real ones because, the fictional villain often becomes a trope, or a symbol to describe real-life situations (as, for instance, when we describe a technological nightmare as a 'Frankensteinian monster', compare indifferent politicians to Nero or dictatorial

figures as Hitler. Here celebrity culture morphs literary and mythic figures onto real life. And what is the real celebrity?—deviance or villainy!

37. 'I can Win', Interview with Charles Shobhraj, *Nepali Times*, No. 217, 8 October–14 October 2004. Available online at http://www. nepalitimes.com/issue/217/Nation/1871.

38. 'Desire to lead a luxurious lifestyle driving youth to crime', *The Hindu*, 2 September 2006. Available online at http://www.hindu. com/2006/09/02/stories/2006090225560300.htm.

39. ATM Centre Guard Held on Cheating Charge', *The Hindu*, 12 July 2007, p. 5.

40. 'Shah Rukh, Gauri Face Legal Notice for "Mannat"', 3 September 2007. Available online at http://in.movies.yahoo.com/070913/211/ 6kpyd.html (downloaded on 13 September 2007).

41. 'Boycott Coke, Aamir Urged', *Times of India*, 13 August 2006. Available online at http://timesofindia.indiatimes.com/article-show/1890538.cms (downloaded on 14 July 2007); 'Aamir Finds Real Life brings Tough Questions', *Daily News and Analysis*, 15 April 2006. Available online at http://www.dnaindia.com/report. asp?NewsID=1024286 (downloaded on 14 July 2007).

42. Prashant Rane, 'Knocked off their Pedestal', *Society*, July 2007, pp. 60–2.

43. *Moviemag*, July 2007, p. 11.

44. It is now possible to do a 'bakra' online. See *http://www.mtvindia. com/breakingnews/14 July 2007*.

5

With Stars in Our Eyes: Consuming Celebrity

I am crazy about Salman Khan...my request is to please give us an exclusive interview with Sallu bhai...[1]

Please feature either of them [Hrithik, Kareena] in Classic Shots...[2]

Please feature Emraan Hashmi in Classic Shots. We love the serial kisser...[3]

Letters such as the above are staple fare in film magazines. They constitute an integral component of celebrity ecology because they demonstrate how celebrities are consumed. Sepia-tinted photographs of film and sports stars stuck inside autorickshaws and taxis. Star calendars and glossy pin-ups for walls. Hand-waving, screaming crowds at celebrity stage shows.

In 2001 the Amitabh Bachchan Fan Association in Kolkata carried out a day-long *puja* prior to selecting a plot to build a temple to him. The Hindi film actress who later shifted to Tamil films, Khushboo, had a temple built for her in Tiruchirapalli (Tamil Nadu), despite the fact that she was born a Muslim. M.G. Ramachandran had a temple built for him years ago in Chennai city. A degree of religiosity informs fans and fandom (Frow 1998: 201).

The Aishwarya Rai-Abhishek Bachchan wedding 'consumed the nation' declared the editor of *Hi! Blitz*, Shalini Sharma.[4]

On 15 August 2004, Independence Day, thousands of devotees performed *pujas* at a temple in Sambalpur (Orissa). The deity? Mahatma Gandhi.[5]

An 86-year old woman, Kanchanban Vaghela of Ahmedabad, fasts to enable Sanjay Dutt to escape imprisonment for his role in the Bombay riots. Even the judge who ruled on Dutt's crime assured him, according to reports of the court proceedings, that he was 'No 1'.[6]

In September 2007, ten years after Diana's death in a car crash, a young girl holds a portrait of the 'people's princess' at Pont de l'Alma, Paris, where Diana died (D'Ancona 2007: 1).

In January 2008, the Telugu film star Dr. Rajasekhar and his family were attacked in Hyderabad city, apparently by *fans* of the reigning super star of Telugu cinema, Chiranjeevi. The reason? Dr. Rajasekhar, when asked if he would join Chiranjeevi's political party, had responded by saying 'no' because he considered Chiranjeevi too inexperienced, a comment that infuriated Chiranjeevi fans.[7]

These are demonstrations of the power of celebrities, our gods and demi-gods today. They indicate how their consumers and followers, rejoice, suffer and even take to violence for their heroes or heroines. But, more importantly, these are demonstrations of the reception of stars and icons by the people.

For *Bigg Boss*, people on the fan site (www.biggboss.in) were asked as to who would win the game. There were inane answers like: 'In my opinion it will be Deepak [Tijori] and Rakhi [Sawant]... but its only the coming days that will decide who will stay and who will go'.[8] Then there was Vijay who gave a more thought-out answer with an analysis of Rakhi Sawant's character in the show: 'Rakhi has to maintain a fine balance and not be seen as a puppet or somebody's pawn... then she has a chance... Otherwise her natural boorishness may cost her her place!'[9] Many of the respondent-users had upwards of 300 posts on the site. Do such texts constitute a part of the ecology of celebrity. What is the link between fan texts and a celebrity?

Celebrity culture is a set of media-driven representations, of people who are seen as worthy of notice, emulation and admiration. But celebrities are also commodities to be consumed, and the *consumption* of SRK or Tendulkar plays as significant a role in the culture of celebrity as the *production* of their celebrity status, especially when the audience produces its own texts about the icons. When the *Washington Post* headlined a story, 'In India's New Consumerism, One Star Has the Most Currency', it captured the multiple dimensions of celebrity culture, such as economic and cultural value, profits and consumption (Wax 2007). It accurately describes SRK, the subject of the piece, as a *commodity* that is available to be consumed.

Texts such as the above mark the *reception* and *consumption* of a star, whether Sachin Tendulkar or SRK. They are *parallel* texts to the films, endorsements, publicity stills, promos that are generated by the media. They are texts that show exactly how the celebrity circulates in public culture.

The audience, the fan, the worshipper, the celebrity stalker respond to the celebrity's iconic power, but they also actively construct the celebrity. They contribute to gossip, to the series or films, to the reviews and to the revenue. It is simplistic to believe that the audience is mindlessly swayed and enchanted by the celebrity. The media is increasingly focused on glamour, youth, power and looks, where even the news report is an excuse for fashion and entertainment. The ephemeral, the strategically mediated real, such as those seen on Reality TV, the scandalous and the arrogant are qualities that circulate in the media, and even become desirable. The audience participates in this by voting for contests, buying fashion products, attending the shows and producing their own fan work. In short, the audience *consumes* the celebrity and celebrity culture is driven by the logic of consumerism, where particular kinds of looks or qualities are marketed for people to buy.

Celebrity culture cannot be understood without examining the role of the audience and the most intense mode of celebrity reception: fans and fandom. Fans are as significant a component of celebrity ecology as the mass media because they reveal the other side of celebrity culture: its consumption.

Constructing Audiences

To see the fan audience as a passive consumer of the celebrity *spectacle* is to minimise the role of the audience in the making of celebrity culture. Spectacle refers to the idea that everything is an event to be looked at and attended to. And a celebrity is the event that everyone watches.

We see fans and audience in *action*—whether it is football hooliganism in England, fan disruption of film shootings or fan mail—suggesting a more active role for the fan audience. In order to look at the role of fan audiences it is useful to employ the 'spectacle/performance' paradigm (Abercrombie and Longhurst 1998).

The audience is a consumer. It adds profits to the film industry, the TV serial, the manufacturing industry. Thus the audience-product—whether the product is a film, a celebrity or a domestic item—relationship is often seen as a *commercial* transaction. This commercial transaction is dependent upon the ability to successfully persuade the audience to remain a spectator and to continue to watch SRK films, a TV serial or *Indian Idol*. The task of the programme producer, film maker or event manager is to hold the attention of sufficient numbers of people for a sufficient length of time. When we speak of a star's charisma, it refers to her or his ability to render large numbers of people spectators—to hold them enthralled by her or his looks, personality and talent.

The relationship between celebrity and audience is one of enthrallment. It is a performance where the celebrity's antics on screen or stage must *captivate* the audience. Glamour, the term used most frequently to describe the celebrity, is the key component of this performance. Incidentally, 'glamour' etymologically meant anything to do with magic and witchcraft:

hence enthrallment or enchantment. This is the performative nature of the spectator-celebrity relationship.

Everything about a celebrity's public appearance and image has to be a performance—*dramatic* and *theatrical*. Even game shows and contests take recourse to drama as a means of engaging the audience's attention. Notice, for instance, the few seconds of silence and non-action before Mini Mathur and K.K. Hussain announce the name of the contestant voted out on *Indian Idol 3*. This is what I call the *about-to* moment. The presenters announce that they are about to declare the name, the camera pans across the faces of the contestants, with many sitting tight-lipped, praying or in various stages of tension, and seconds tick by before they dramatically call out the name. The *about-to* moment is theatre where the suspense is built up so that the audience will not go away. It focalises the attention of the spectator on the events unfolding. Then there are the behind-the-scenes programmes that take you into the everyday lives of the contestants. All of it is *theatre*, and theatre that emphasises the human angle of the contest. Thus participants reveal their dreams and aspirations, their emotional states, their anxieties and their despair. (What Gloria-Jean Masciarotte has appropriately termed spectacular emotionalism.) (Masciarotte 2004: 251) It is *emotion picture* as nothing else. *Koffee with Karan* and other talk shows become dramatic in their format of presentation with the *about-to* moment: what is *about to* be revealed about the celebrity. The *about-to* moment is *heightened drama*. who is the celebrity announced so dramatically by Karan Johar, what *will* the audience discover *next*?

Such dramatic moments are meant to heighten our interest in the characters and individuals we see on the stage or the screen. The programme carefully organises the spectators' dispositions towards the contestants or the celebrities. We are told they are popular, they have failed this recent round, the jury looks unhappy with them, that the audience has voted for them. *Then* we are shown the participants and the celebrities themselves. The smiling Madhuri Dixit, the worried

Deepali anticipating a negative comment from the abrasive Anu Malik on *Indian Idol 3*, the diffident Rakhi Sawant, the suavely arrogant star-power of SRK on *Koffee with Karan* and the trying-to-be-ordinary Shakti Kapoor on *Life Ban Jaye*, the anxious moments with zoom-ins of the participants before Bachchan or SRK announces whether the answer is right or wrong on *KBC*. These are dramatic formulae that ensure the spectator's attention.

The media treats the audience as potential consumers of the celebrity product, a process that entails feeding the imagination and emotions of the audience through such theatre. The audience is constructed as consumer because retailing celebrities is a commercial proposition, a profit-making venture.

The audience is offered the spectacle of the celebrity—the style, the lifestyle, the fashion, the appearance, the scandal and the social scene. We are asked to imagine possessing a similar kind of life: 'you-can-be-like-this-too'. The media thrives on such a construction of the audience: given enough promotion of celebrity products, the audience will consume even more because the individual aspires to acquire the life and style of her or his chosen celebrity.

However, this does not make the audience an unthinking, passive consumer; the audience is a discerning one, picking and rejecting celebrities as it does their films, behaviour and events. Fans and audiences do accept media-driven images and discourses about celebrities, but it is never simply quiescent. It (and here I run the risk of homogenizing audiences, though regional, linguistic, gendered variations do exist *within* audiences) does possess an *agency*. The rejection of the reigning super star SRK in *Paheli* (2005) is a case in point. Not even his enormous star power could draw audiences after the first week. Amitabh Bachchan has had his flops, and Sachin Tendulkar his detractors. Despite the massive publicity around Sanjay Leela Bhansali's *Saawariya* (2007), the audience across India rejected the film. All this indicates an audience that might be, on one level, constructed by the media, but is never reduced to passive acceptance. It indicates that the celebrity media and audience relationship is more complex than we can visualise. On the one hand the media instils a desire for celebrities and circulates icons for consumption, fuelling and channelizing audience desires in the process. On the other, the audience does not always willingly accept these icons and discourses, but participates in its consumption of particular celebrities and even creates its own products' as this chapter argues.

The audience actively participates in the production of itself as a fan audience. It engages with the celebrity images directed at it, and generates meanings that lead to even greater consumption of the celebrity images. However, this is not the only active role of the fan audience.

The fan audience is a mode of social interaction, sometimes cutting across class and regional affiliations. Cricket and Sachin Tendulkar, are consumed across the demographic spectrum and across the subcontinent. The construction of a fan audience relies on this cultural variety, and the celebrity can be seen as a force that achieves a temporary unifying effect in this diversity. Such a construction is determined in a major way by the medium used.

Driving through any metropolis now, we are often distracted by large hoardings. As though these still images were not enough, Hyderabad city, following in the illustrious footsteps of NYC was to have LED movie screens at 15 specific points featuring models and fashion on a *moving* screen (Chunduri 2006).[10] Arguably, such digital screens with moving images only extend the narrative patterns of billboards and hoardings. However, the implications of telecasting events live on such screens on the road are slightly different. Traffic updates on the FM radio, daily news uploaded on your mobile phone, downloadable films all mean that something is *enhanced*. What is enhanced is the audience *experience*.

In earlier eras the day was mostly divided into work and rest. With the television another segment was carved out of the day—TV time. Time spent watching TV is now a regular feature of households across the world. The most insistent and omniscient medium of the twentieth century is surely the TV.

Extending the TV-viewing time and experience are such hoard-ings and the bombardment by images from all sides, at all times, in various forms, such as advertisements, propaganda, news, information, entertainment and SMS updates on mobile phones. We are a perpetual audience because images, adver-tisements and propaganda are constantly in the background, and often in the foreground, of our everyday life, even when we are not paying concentrated attention to them. Or, in John Urry's terms, people are much of the time tourists whether they like it or not (Urry 1990: 82). In other words the proliferation of mass media in our everyday lives means we live in the age of spectacle.

We live in an environment of the mediated quasi-interaction (Abercrombie and Longhurst 1998: 64–8). We do not meet the stars face-to-face, the original form of interaction, but through a heavily mediated interaction. It must be kept in mind that the performance of the star is not targeted at a specific audience or group but to a *diffused* audience *out there* (Abercrombie and Longhurst 1998: 68–76). That is, the audience for any performance now, whether it is a cricket match telecast over many channels or the Concert for Diana, is *potentially unlimited and unknowable*. Unlike the circus or the theatre where the audience is present right there and can be seen, described and identified, contemporary audiences for the Filmfare Awards for Sunita Williams' return to earth or for the presidential swearing-in is amorphous, diffuse and unknowable. Thus SRK or Karan Johar point at us from the screen during their show (*KBC* and *Koffee with Karan* respectively) but cannot be certain as to who is watching them.

In the age of mass media, such televised spectacles reaching across geography and time find a diffused audience, unknow-able and unlimited. The key element of this heavily medi-ated society of spectacle, such as we see now in contemporary metropolitan culture, is that the people are an *audience* at all times. That is, being a member of an audience is not an option or a matter of choice any more; one is always (in) the audience. We spend more time consuming images from mass media in the home and in public now. Indeed, mass media images are now a part of everyday life—driving to work, walking on the street or reading the newspaper in the morning. We are also subjected to performances and media images on the cell phone, the hoarding, the radio, the pavement and the television.

What does such a mediated quasi-interaction mean for celebrity culture? To begin with, it generates a central paradox. The celebrity is both, right here with her or his fan audience and is yet very distant. The celebrity is a part of the fan audience's everyday life and as remote from it as imaginable. The celebrity is thus *both intimate and distant*. We know they are with us (inside autorickshaws, staring down at us from hoardings, the sound of their voice on radios and portable music systems, in ads) at every moment, and yet they are never with us. The original performance of SRK in his film is removed from his fans because they will never see him at the actual shoot. Yet promos now regularly include 'the making of...', aired on TV, allowing some kind of deeper access into it.

This simultaneous proximity and distancing enhances the celebrity's value. Mediated spectacles such as the ones mentioned above successfully underscore the social distance between the celebrity and the audience, while assuring the latter that the star is very real. Descriptions of their lifestyles achieve the same result. They make the stars more human when the audience is fed information, some of it unbelievably trivial, about their homes, clothes or relationships while at the same time sending out the message that only they can live like *this*.

The diffused audience is created through constant *performance*. Baz Kershaw has argued that the increased role of media in everyday life today means that performance is inserted into everyday life (Kershaw 1996). Performance, as Erving Goffman defined it, is 'all activity of an individual which occurs during a period marked by his continuous presence before a particular set of observers and which has some influence on the observers' (Goffman 1969: 19). These definitions draw attention to not only the role-playing by the performer (in this case the star) but also to the *act* of observation (in this case the mediated spectacle).

The constant representation of images and spectacle on our screen, eye and imagination today, transforms us into *perpetual* spectators and transforms all events into performances for consumption. Indeed it could be a truism to state that everyday performance is possible because of the screen or the mass media. Whatever SRK or Sania Mirza is doing—shopping, dining out or holidaying—they are (media) watched. They are always playing a role because even their everyday life becomes a performance that is then telecast or printed for consumers, including their fan audience. Hence their hand waves to the crowds, the smile and the careful attention to their wardrobe. Even mundane events thus become *performances*, and add to the aura of the star because they are disseminated to a diffused audience across territories. In addition to being a society of spectacle, we now have a society of performance. Theatricality and performance, including the ceremonial hand wave of the celebrity, is now part of our everyday life. Stars are on 24×7, and this perpetual hyper-visibility is a central feature of celebrity ecology.

The ordinary-as-celebrity, linked to the demotic turn in celebrity culture explored in the preceding chapters, also results in some interesting changes to the nature of audience, spectacle and performance. MTV or any other channel takes to the streets, interviewing people, filming them with or without their knowledge. Mobile phone films shot by amateurs transform the person on the street (previously only an audience to the celebrity-as-spectacle) into the performer. Thus the common woman or man is also a performer as a result of the mass media's interest, however fleeting, in her or his life. *Consumers of culture become producers of culture, people who watch celebrities flit across their screens and offering sound bites now themselves play this role of (short-lived) celebrities with their opinions being disseminated through the media.* The mass media revolution therefore alters the spectacle/audience paradigm by *transforming the audience itself into the performance/performer or spectacle.* In many cases, of course, this transformation reverses the public/private structure of performance and spectacle, when the person's moods, expression or action are caught, without their knowledge, on screen. Private acts and emotions become public spectacle, even though these were not intended as roles for public consumption. With the demotic turn, even the person in the street has the opportunity or runs the risk of having her or his everyday, conventional and personal acts becoming a public spectacle.

Fans and Fandom

As *Indian Idol 3* ran through its contest on Sony TV, the organisers held a Fantastic Fan contest for the TV audience. The organisers suggested that the fans had very real power:

Share with us pictures, videos or a write up about what you are doing to help your favourite win Indian Idol. And let the world know how powerful you actually are![11]

By giving voting power to the audience, thereby enabling them to decide the next celebrity, and encouraging fan activity, *Indian Idol 3* acknowledged the power of fans to alter the course of events.

The transformation of a contestant into a celebrity requires the validation of the audience. The audience's stake in the elimination or winning of the stars is once again a democratisation of celebrity culture, where it is not the contestant's lineage, connections or wealth but her or his fan following in the public sphere that determines her or his success and stardom.[12] Emon and Parleen, Deepali and Charu, all had their own fan following as evidenced by the letters and responses, even as many of these contestants bow out.[13]

Fans are a response to the media-driven system that constructs stars. They accept the meanings generated by the celebrity text, but are not mere passive consumers of the star. As we shall see, fans construct their own text and generate their own meanings of the star-text. This is fan-text, something that may be derived from the star's persona, role or achievement, but is not necessarily the construction of the media industry that surrounds the star. This fan-text reveals the processes through which an audience *consumes* a celebrity.

The term 'fan', also connected etymologically to 'fanatic' and 'fancy', originally referred to an excessively enthusiastic man at the temple. Fancy was used to refer to the patrons of prize-fighting (Cashmore 2006: 79). The term thus gestures at both an emotional attachment to particular icons or beliefs *and* a sense of collectivity. Indeed it could be argued that emotional intimacy with the audience or fans is a marker of an individual's authentic celebrity status. Fans constitute the audience for the celebrity-spectacle. There would be no celebrities without audiences and fans.

The point is, the structure of the celebrity-text may be a media-generated spectacle. But the *meaning* of the celebrity-text is generated by *real* people (Franco 2006: 269). Fans generate an entire culture *around* their chosen celebrity by making newer and more diverse meanings from the principal text. Fandom is therefore a significant component of celebrity ecology, for without fans to make sense of them, celebrities would not *be* celebrities. It is important to note that the circulation and consumption of celebrities occurs from below: at the level of real people who are well below the celebrities in terms of class, social and cultural power.

When we recall the crowds mourning Diana, many weeping openly, or those waiting to catch a glimpse of their favourite stars at film shoots and award ceremonies, it comes home to us that fans are not simply about adoration of the celebrity. Fandom involves a degree of very personal, emotional involve-ment with the subject of adoration (Sandvoss 2005: 8). The emphasis on *emotional* involvement is something to be kept in mind because it often results in the creation of a distinct *text* in celebrity culture.

Fan cultures are dependent and draw upon their chosen celebrity but are not restricted to them. That is, fandom may draw upon the life, images and work of their chosen celebrity but is not entirely determined by them. Thus fans undertake philanthropic work in the name of their hero (a common feature in fan associations in Hyderabad, for example).

Fans watch, re-watch and often recreate the scenes of their favourite celebrities. They are witnesses to the celebrity's performances, often making up more than just an audience: they take out processions to celebrate their hero's success, to announce his new film, or even haunt studios and sets. They constitute a community in itself. They also, very often, create a massive corpus of *their own texts* (fan-texts), such as commentaries, opinions, songs, fiction, criticism, letters, about their chosen celebrities.

The fan is engaged in what has been called a para-social relationship with people she or he may never meet (Turner 2004: 92–4). This is not a pejorative term, even though people sometimes substitute real relationships with such surrogate or imagined ones. The para-social relationship is a kind of intimacy generated through the mass media. While normal relationships require face-to-face meetings and interaction, the para-social relationship a fan has with SRK or any other celebrity is almost entirely based, usually, on watching his films, media images and affective responses of the viewer to the images. Furthermore, as Chris Rojek has argued, the para-social relationship becomes necessary in increasingly fragmented societies where they help battle isolation and loneliness (Rojek 2001: 52).

Although the term para-social captures the semi-illusionary nature of the relationship between celebrities and fans it does not quite help us see the often crucial emotional, social and even spiritual dimensions of fandom and the fan-celebrity link. For example, the term cannot even begin to describe the anguish expressed by people across the world at Princess Diana's death. Was that simply a para-social relationship, an illusion shared by millions?

I propose *extimacy* as a term that better captures the relationship of the adoring fan and the adored celebrity. Extimacy, created by adding the prefix 'ex' from 'exterior' to 'intimacy', is a term used in psychoanalysis to describe the complex nature of the inside/outside relationship. The completely strange Other is both outside and yet inside. Thus it is neither completely outside nor inside because it has been internalized (Evans 1996).[14] Extimacy refers to this complex relationship between the outside and inside, the container and the contained. This is the relationship of the fan and the celebrity—it is what can be called 'intersubjective' where the notions, images and desire of the celebrity by the fan are internalized. Although the star is a definite material object outside, she or he constitutes a very real psychological state of adoration for the fan. For the fan the star is no stranger out there, but somebody who has been internalized. The Other is intimate here.

SRK might be a star whom you will never meet. Veerappan might be the daring villain you admired. However, the affective (emotional) investment one makes,[15] as fan letters and writings capture, but only in limited ways, since emotional responses are not always made public, internalizes the celebrity for the fan. Celebrities, especially sports celebrities, become sources of inspiration and their successes become the fan's success. 'When you win, you win all hearts', declares a Sania Mirza fan.[16] Or here is Sandy Bachra writing about seeing SRK at Warwick Castle:

> As he smiled at the crowd I felt my heart melt…As he held the sword high and cut the ribbon I felt as if I was in heaven. I had waited so long…too long…for such a perfect moment…
>
> He approached us slowly and I jerked my arm forward as I held my postcard and pen in front of him to sign. After a little wait he took somebody else's pen and placed his name on my card. I felt as if my journey was complete and I finally had something to treasure for the rest of my life. As I pulled back I watched him interacting with people while I carefully examined every part of him. For yet he had not taken any photos next to fans but after pleading with him we managed to get him to pause from the hectic signing he was doing and got him to take a photo with a little girl who's birthday it was going to be the day after. That small sacrifice of his made me realize how much he appreciated the love and support we gave him. He spent a great deal of his time signing autographs, interact-

ing with fans; I even noticed him answer a phone call for one of his fans. He was what I called my sweetheart.

As he left us, I was so energetic and just wanted to scream and shout about the fact he had acknowledged my presence. At such a young age my dream had already come true; I was one of the lucky few.[17]

The degree of emotional involvement and investment this fan makes is hardly 'para' anything. For her it is clearly very *real*, and the actual face-to-face meeting with her adored celebrity adds to the investment in the celebrity. Such affective investment in an external individual effectively brings the outsider inside.

This process of internalization might go some way in explaining the obsessive behaviour of some fans (stalking) or celebrity-related suicides.[18] Extimacy carried to its extremes is the relationship stalkers have with the celebrity object of their unwanted attention. In the case of the stalker, the celebrity's public face is what drives the obsessed stalker. The stalker has internalized the image of the celebrity.

Fandom is, according to several critics, an index of narcissism (Abercrombie and Longhurst 1998: 77–98). In Stephen King's *Misery* (1987), the deranged nurse declares: 'I am your Number One fan' to the writer. The statement is as much about the celebrity as it is about the adoring fan. If the fan internalizes the celebrity in an act of extimacy, it follows that the fan sees the celebrity as an extension of her or his self. For the fan, following the celebrity is an essential part of her or his life. Fans, especially, in their productions, are involved in an imagined performance in the presence of others. The intention is to convey the extent of adoration, to show fanhood *to the fan-world* through exhibitions of intimate knowledge, emotional attachment and commitment. An extension of the fan's self is an act of self-reflection—seeing herself or himself and the object of affection as reflective and constitutive of each other. This self-reflection occurs in a *social environment with other fans*. Every fan performs for herself or himself as much as for other fans, in order to demonstrate the degree of adoration: '*I* am your number one fan'.

However, such public expressions as Sandy Bachra's are not always the norm in fandom. Cornel Sandvoss argues for another kind of self-reflection: not between fans and their environment but between the fan and the object of fandom (Sandvoss 2005: 98–122).

Wearing a Salman Khan or Dhoni hairstyle is the appropriation of the loved object by the fan. During the 1980s, Amitabh Bachchan's hairstyle was *the* fashion statement. During the cricket World Cup 2007, Reliance marketed the Indian team's colours (t-shirts) at all its outlets. These are forms of impersonation when the youth imitate Salman Khan's styles, a Beckham Tee with his number, or wear fashion accessories popularised by celebrities and film stars. Sandvoss proposes that such a process indicates the internalization of an external object. The loved object of fandom *becomes a part of the self, a textual extension of the self.* This is an interesting mode of looking at the fan-celebrity interaction. It suggests that people who mime, or resemble, celebrities somehow suggest a *personal relationship* with their fan object or celebrity. Thus the celebrity is a part of the self of the fan. The search for parallels and similarities between fans and their fan objects is clearly an example of extimacy, and is, I believe, a key mode of celebrity reception.

The search for affinity rather than similarity (though there is always a great demand for star look-alikes, as we know) is based on the need of the fan to be as like the fan object as possible. The celebrity, interestingly, is seen as an extension of the fan's self in a process of identificatory fantasising or narcissistic self-reflection: 'see, SRK is like me'.

This identificatory fantasy born out of the extimacy of the fan-celebrity relationship is also a performance where the fan audience becomes a performer, either private or public.

Fans often draw upon the celebrity to craft their own identity. This is, however, not an entirely accurate description of the fan. Fans, as we shall see, produce fan texts. Fan production—songs, fanzines, fan club work—allows the fan to become a celebrity herself or himself. With the Internet individuals can bypass the media industry and set up their own fan sites, rendering them producers and celebrities in their own right. That is, fan individuals and groups need not, now, depend on expensive equipment or visibility time on TV to become celebrities for their fandom. They can produce fan texts and become visible on their own. The State Wide Chiranjeevi Youth Welfare Association's campaign to pledge eye donation has generated a different kind of fan production—the social cause. The association's official stationery carries the legend, 'donate eyes, live twice'.[19] Such fan productions do have a social impact, and thus cannot be dismissed as crazed fandom. Photographs of stars shaking hands with fans, visiting them, or interacting with them are common features now. These are acts that render the fans celebrities. Thus R. Swamy Naidu, the Secretary of the State Wide Chiranjeevi Youth Welfare Association, received an award from Chiranjeevi (22 August 1996), the Telugu film superstar, for social service. The photograph of the award ceremony transformed Naidu from being a fan into a celebrity himself, receiving the award and recognition from the star.[20] Likewise, Avik Pal Bhowmick, who sketched SRK finds recognition in terms of his own photograph on the SRK fan club's website (www.vluvshahrukhkhan.com)— once again the fan becomes a celebrity. There is, as Matt Hills points out, a *hierarchy of fans* (Hills 2006: 111–8). People like Swamy Naidu or Avik Pal Bhowmick achieve recognition for their fan productions, knowledge about their chosen celebrity or contribution to society in the name of their celebrity. Within fan sites, therefore, we recognize names as regular contributors to fan mail and other writing.

Thus to simply see fans as derived from and *secondary* to celebrity culture is not entirely accurate. Fans may themselves become celebrities, becoming known to fellow fans and perhaps to the wider world through their fan productions.

In some cases, fans keep alive a series independent of the original. These are cult TV programmes where *particular figures are treated as celebrities only by their fan audiences*. These are what Matt Hills calls subcultural celebrities— individuals with restricted celebrity status (Hills 2003: 61).

Fan cultures keep celebrities alive well after their original TV series has ended. *Star Trek*, the cult TV series, generated another parodic TV series, *Galaxy Quest* (1978–1982) made by the original series' audiences.

Fan cultures and community-formation has been massively altered and facilitated through the Internet. Online fan communities exist in India and Hollywood for practically every film star and all major sports stars, and constitute a major subcultural phenomenon (Pullen 2000). Online fan work is an extension into *another* realm, but one that is as significant in terms of community formation and civil society, of those acts that is already in existence offline. However, certain crucial differences exist. Online fan activity opens up the space of fan culture. Women, especially, find it more suitable to express their opinions or desires online because cyberspace ensures a degree of anonymity. It is also a mode of constructing a collective or community identity in cyberspace, where fellow fans meet and friendships develop. Thus social disadvantages that proceed from their gender roles are erased through cyberculture. In some cases, large online fan communities also give rise to smaller, more private networks which function as women's support groups (Clerc 2002).

Fan Production

My five-and-a-half-year-old son enacts battle scenes with his collection of Power Rangers and Transformers, often explaining to me elaborate plots involving bad and good Rangers, mixed with models of Batman, dinosaurs and assorted Hot Wheels cars. With his slightly older friend, Andrew, he sometimes arranges assorted animals, including dinosaurs, in military formation, presumably enacting war scenarios.

Clueless as to the original plots of both Power Rangers and Transformers, I rely on his version of events. Efforts to explain to him that these are fictions (celefiction was not a term I tried out then!) proved futile. It then dawned on me, as a slow adult, that for him, his creations of storylines with these characters were *real*. My son was in fact *producing fan fiction*.[21]

Fans, as consumers of the celebrity-commodity are producers in their own right. Fan production is perhaps the best illustration of how the celebrity is received, circulated and consumed by society. Fan production shifts the focus from the modes and technologies through which celebrities are produced by the media industry to the modes through which fans

1. generate meaning of the celebrity,
2. create their own texts around the celebrity,
3. construct a community of like-minded people,
4. empower themselves.

Children enact scenes from films and play the roles of their various superheroes. Thus the celefiction becomes a part of everyday life and leisure. Celefictions become real in the sense they constitute the games actually played out by children. What is interesting is that very often these games are inventions of the child fan, involving the celefiction in situations and scenes imagined by the child, and which may be very far removed from the script of the TV serial or programme of the original celefiction. Thus games with toy models of Power Rangers are narratives that generate a parallel, non-official storyline exclusively produced by the fans. Material products such as autographed cricket bats and memorabilia are also consumed and inserted into personal meaning systems. 'Ideal for Any Indian Cricket Fan' declares www.cricket.com, announcing a 'Mini Cricket Bat Signed by Sachin Tendulkar'. Thus the miniature bat, with *no* practical sporting use whatsoever, becomes a part of the fantasies of individuals.

The celefiction, whether Power Rangers or Barbie dolls, is re-interpreted by the fan and new meanings generated. The production is often very *material* in the sense that the celefiction is dressed up, altered, made to act as part of the fan's everyday leisure. This is *fan production*.

Fan production can be of three types, as outlined by Fiske (1992). *Semiotic production* is the creation of meaning by fans through a process of reading. This is the result of a personal interaction with the celebrity text, and is the meaning generated by the fan through viewing the celebrity's movies and performances. Thus, reviews and commentaries that draw upon personal interpretation of a film on fan sites could be described as semiotic fan production.

Enunciative production is the social interaction that is achieved through the fans' consumption of the celebrity. Central to fan culture is fan exchanges. 'Fan Connect' on *www.vluvshahrukhkhan.com* enables fans to exchange news, gossip and opinions about their chosen celebrity. This exchange also generates an enormous amount of textual material—photographs, reviews, discussions, songs—in many genres. The regular exchanges between fans, the sharing of information, generates texts of various kinds and must be treated as a part of both fan consumption. Since these texts draw upon earlier media circulated texts, and fan production because they create a community based on their common adoration. Communication here is central to the formation of the fan community. Online fan sites and the new technologies of communication have greatly enhanced the interaction among fans. The 'Fan House' on *www.vluvshahrukhkhan.com* is an example of this intra-group communication that creates texts.

With the new technologies of information, like the Internet, enunciative fan production has entered a new era. We now have a massive amount of *information* generated by fans and designed for public access. On *www.tendulkar.co.in* a Sachin Tendulkar fan site, his complete career statistics are displayed, though it has not been updated since February 2006. One distinguishing feature about fan sites is that they provide personal information about their stars. For Tendulkar, for instance, *www.tendulkar.co.in* provides information about Tendulkar's and his family. Details about father's profession, the mother-in-law's name, his children, his preferred charities—all this is easily available. There is also a substantial amount of visual material. In the case of fan sites of Hollywood stars these are invariably highly sexualised (see Lambiase 2003, for a study).

Zoom's *Bollywood Newzflash* provided a list of celebrities present at Karan Johar's birthday party—Abhishek, SRK, Salman Khan (26 May 2007). *Filmfare* in its '9 to 5 with Kareena Kapoor [sic]' (May 2007: 86–7) takes us through the day with the star. This is how the magazine introduces the column:

> We all want a glimpse into the lives of our stars. Even what they do when they're waiting for their shot. What they wear when they report to the shoot. And how long they take to get ready... the inside scoop in the lives of your favourite star.

This inside scoop involves providing information that Karan Johar has idli-sambar for breakfast and that Kareena, Manish Malhotra and Shahid Kapoor often have dinner at his place. This kind of information retailing is central to the consumption of the celebrity. It enables the making of a para-social relation with the star because the fan believes she or he knows the star intimately.

Fans provide a massive database of details about their chosen celebrity. It could be argued that fan sites are a parallel source of information about celebrities, where information both private and personal about the celebrity is a necessary component of the fans. I term this *vernacular information*. This is not to relegate it to a secondary status. It is vernacular (etymologically it means domestic or native) because there is no *official* sanction for any of this information and there is no confirmation or denial of this information.[22] That is, one assumes the information is true in the absence of any proof on the fan site or in the fanzine. *Vernacular information is native, localised, often impromptu, subjective, informal and possesses high affective (emotional) component and is in contrast with the more cultivated, perhaps literary and learned information of official website information put out by the star's offices and publicity machinery.* Unregulated, as opposed to strictly monitored official sites and information, and subversive at times,[23] vernacular information is crucial in generating communities that are often independent of the star's marketing.

Vernacular information is constituted by the accumulation of extra information that may have nothing to do with the celebrity's actual career or profession. Thus, it is not necessary in the general scheme of things to know that Sachin Tendulkar's father-in-law, Anand Mehta, is a paediatrician by profession. It is in no way connected to Tendulkar's success story on the cricket field. It is possible that in the case of ascribed celebrities, which, as we have seen, is celebrity status following from lineage, this kind of vernacular information counts as professional information. As an instance, look at the second-order information for Abhishek Bachchan.

For Abhishek Bachchan the welcome note on *http://www. abhishekbachchan.org/abhishek* states:

First referred to as nothing more than a shadow of his legendary father due to early blunders, he is now ready to write his own story and become a legend himself! (21 May 2007)

Then the biographical section opens with:

Abhishek Bachchan: the name has been the reason for endless speculations. Will he? Won't he? Ever since he returned from his Swiss school and was spotted at functions towering over his petite mother and standing almost shoulder-to-shoulder with his larger-than-life father, he has had movie moghuls flocking to his side. Just about everyone who was anyone had a project lined up for the Small B. And no one had any doubts that he would follow in his father's footsteps.

The rhetoric focusses exclusively on lineage. The code 'small B' as opposed to 'Big B', the nickname by which Amitabh Bachchan is known to all Indians and several people abroad, marks this lineage.

Enunciative fan production can also take the form of material cultures based on celebrity texts. Fashion codes adopted by fans, Salman Khan's hairstyle in *Tere Naam* that became a rage, and then Dhoni's long hair, are examples of enunciative fan production. Thus celebrity culture thrives on enunciative text productions *that incorporate the star into the everyday life of the fan(s).*

There is also fan *textual production* where the fans produce an enormous amount of poetry, fiction or songs devoted to and building upon their celebrity. This is the most fascinating of the fan productions.

In the Euro-American contexts fanzines and fan writing often involve the production of stories involving celefiction. *Star Trek* fan fiction is the most popular of these.[24] Fans in this case re-read the original series and its stories before creating their own.[25] Thus fans are not passive consumers here. They are active *producers* of stories. The audience has become a producer.

Celebrities, whether individual actors or actresses or TV serials, clearly help generate parallel literary and artistic productions by fans. Ashok Banker's retelling of the *Ramayana* is a hugely successful publishing project. Incidentally, Banker is also the editor of a new magazine, *Epic India*. This magazine now publishes *fan fiction* that builds on Banker's *Ramayana*, but seeks to, in its own words, 'fill the void of 13 years between *"Demons of Chitrakut"* and *"Armies of Hanuman"*, books 3 and 4 of the series respectively'. The tale, *Warriors of Dandaka*, by Pushpak Karniak (identified and spelt as Pushpak *Karnick* on his blog at www.bloggers.com), is explicitly identified as fan fiction, 'devoted to the *Ramayana* series by amcha [our] bhai Ashok Banker' in the magazine.[26]

The most popular pair of the Hindi film screen from the 1990s, SRK-Kajol (*Baazigar, Karan Arjun, DDLJ, Kuch Kuch Hota Hai, K3G*) has its own dedicated fan fiction. *Kabhi Na Kabhi Pyaar To Hoga*, scripted by 'sweet_shal' (*http:// www.srk-kajol.net/fanfic/viewstoryphp?sid=35&chapter= 1*). A detailed plot of the story is available, and reads exactly like the script for a romantic movie. The celefiction of the century, Harry Potter, commands his own fan fiction (*http://www. harrypotterfanfiction.com/viewstory.php?psid=218583*).

Fan fiction can also use other forms. Here is a poetic example [sic]:

> I know someone
> Who is so innocent and Cute
> The eyes that he got
> Has capture me in my dreamt
> He got the sweetest smile
> Because his smile make everybody dream of him all the time
> Those innocent face he do have
> Make all the girls go down and love him more
> He isn't handsome as other actors
> But there is something inside of him that made attracted us
> Sometimes IM wondering what is so special about him
> But until now I can't find the answer of it
> And only one person who can do me this way
> That is only My Lovely Shahrukh Khan

This is one of the many poems on www.vluvshahrukhkhan. com, a Shah Rukh Khan fan site. Other fan sites also carry similar material.

Fan texts help generate an identity for the fan, an identity that might be linked to that of the celebrity but is not restricted to it. Thus individuals writing poems to SRK or Tendulkar might acquire an identity as an 'SRK fan' but is much more than just this. Among fan circles and communities, this individual is also the *poet* who wrote.

Poems such as the one quoted above, stories about their chosen celebrities, fan artwork, gossip and production schedules (most film star celebrity fan sites have a list of their star's forthcoming films). There are letters and postings to bulletin boards on every fan site. These are personal notes that suggest an emotional involvement with the celebrity's life and career. Sugandh Juneja on www.vluvshahrukhkhan.com writes:

> I have met him 5 times n he is the sweetest person I could've ever met in my life. He is just simply too good n he even let me play with Aryan for 35 minutes now can nobody beat that?

Raveena on the same 'Thoughts on Shahrukh Khan' describes herself as 'obsessed about shahrukh [sic]'.

Fan exchanges such as these are also *performances*. From being a mere passive audience, these fans have become producers in their own right, creating fan texts that are then circulated among others. These are textual performances that also encode emotional, highly personal performances of loyalty, affection and admiration. It is possible to argue that such exchanges and fan textual productions are *imaginative appropriations* of the celebrity performer by an audience that then becomes the performer. Thus, through this process of appropriation, the spectacle and performance distinctions get blurred, even if the fan fiction does not acquire the status of a celebrity text. The audience-as-performer, also seen in the screaming crowds at concerts, the hand-waving cheering spectators at sports events, is the construction of a new order of celebrity-audience interaction where the audience acquires the power and the ability to generate its own meanings through its performance.

Fan productions can be subversive because the fan generates her or his own meaning other than the one intended by the media machine. Denial of Elvis' death, and the claims that he is alive somewhere, for instance, subverts the media's widespread details of the fact of his death. Reports of Tendulkar's poor form elicit responses from fans that demonstrate their continuing belief in his ability. Such fan productions often become counter-narratives to the main text of celebrity culture.

Fan exchanges enable the building of a community. Revolving around the admiration and affection for the celebrity, we can see the community as a new mode of social interaction. It constitutes a new dimension of the public sphere minus the face-to-face interaction, though fans might get to meet each other offline. They use their chosen celebrity's successes, interests or failures to start a discussion that thus brings people together. 'Celebrity chatter', as Ellis Cashmore calls it, is a 'universal cultural currency' (Cashmore 2006: 87). It is important to realise that such celebrity chatter is often a community-building device (communication and community have, etymologically at least, common origins).

Fan production, especially with online work, empowers them. Their consumption of popular icons such as SRK or Sania Mirza leads to a sense of fulfilment—that they know more about their celebrity than anybody else. Fan productions must therefore be seen not only as markers of the fans' affective investment in their celebrity and community-building but also as a means of empowerment by setting themselves as distinct (even above) other, ordinary viewers of SRK and Sania Mirza through their epistemological familiarity with the stars. In the face of a massive media industry that ceaselessly produces celebrity images which are therefore mass and indistinctive, fan productions become more *singular, specific* and *intimate*, written with a degree of specialized knowledge and emotional investment, with the text of the production (as in the case of children) constructing an imagined role of the celebrity or celefiction in their personal lives. Fan productions are often the result of the extimacy that informs fan-celebrity relationship.

Clearly then celebrity culture is not simply about the media-driven production of cults, personalities and stars. Celebrity culture is an inherently unstable phenomenon because it relies partly upon the reception of these cults, personalities and stars. Celebrity culture is a *transaction* between the mediated image and the audience. Audience reception and consumption resulting in fan production determines the longevity of a celebrity. Celefictions like Harry Potter or Mickey Mouse are not only long-lived because of the extraordinary marketing mechanisms but because die-hard fans and adorers keep them alive. The celebrity occupies this grey zone between plotted production and a relatively autonomous consumption.

The celebrity's power depends upon the careful negotiations of spectacle and performance and the orchestration of their affect. Their dispersal into multiple domains ensures their wider reach and longevity, sometimes well *after* their specialised role (as film star or sports personality). They have entertainment value and marketability. They also serve social

❖ *Seeing Stars*

functions where they represent a nation or culture's values and beliefs. They possess considerable power when they turn to social issues and activism, and thereby move celebrity culture *out from the entertainment domain into the political one*. And, the linkage of the media-entertainment complex with politics, politicians who are media-savvy, media barons with political stakes and roles, political events that are heavily mediated for audience consumption, means that entertainment possesses considerable political power. Celebrities widen the scope of politics and its consciousness-raising dimension by their presence and activism.[27]

This book has emphasised the fact that celebrity culture has to be read at various levels, from mediated constructions, ritualised formats, spectacular (re)presentations (scandalous, heroic) to consumption, where each level merges into others, and where each contributes to the celebrity in complement with others.

Notes

1. *Filmfare*, April 2007, p. 16.
2. *Filmfare*, April 2007, p. 16.
3. *Filmfare*, May 2007, p. 14.
4. *Hi! Blitz*, May 2007, p. 18.
5. 'They All Worship Gandhi at a Temple', Press Trust of India, 16 August 2004. Available online at http://www.expressindia.com/news/fullstory.php?newsid=35087 (downloaded on 15 September 2007).
6. Kartikeya, 'You are No 1, keep the faith: Judge', *The Times of India*, 1 August 2007, p. 1. The number of letters expressing shock, faith in the judiciary and, dismay on the Dutt case decision (*The Hindu*, 3 August, 2007, p. 12) testifies to the spectacular nature of celebrity trials.
7. 'Rajasekhar's Car Stoned, Daughters Injured', *The Hindu*, 29 January 2008, p. 1.
8. 'Big Fan of Big Boss', www.biggboss.in (posted 20/11/2006).
9. 'Big Fan of Big Boss', www.biggboss.in (posted 20/11/2006).

10. 'Beware of Digital Danger', *The Hindu*, 28 November 2006, http://www.hindu.com/2006/11/28/stories/2006112815620300.htm. 25 July 2007.
11. http://indianidol.sify.com/contest/ (downloaded on 31 July 2007).
12. This interactive form of the contest where the audience votes for particular contestants has had interesting side-effects: the show's judges have often been unhappy with the audience's choice (in June both Alisha Chinai and Javed Akhtar expressed their surprise at the audience votes). Yet another kind of interactive audience is that in quiz shows such as *KBC*, where better-educated or better-informed audience members often help the contestant with answers.
13. At a personal level we know at least one couple who named their new born daughter Deepali after the programme!
14. The term comes from the psychoanalyst Jacques Lacan. See Evans (1996).
15. I adopt the term 'affective investment' from J. Franco (2006).
16. 'Topgun Ronnie', posted on 19 February 2006 at http://www.sania-mirza.net/forums/viewtopic.php?t=291 (downloaded on 28 July 2007). Another form of consumption is the creation of sports subcultural groups (see Wheaton 2007).
17. 'King Khan at Warwick Castle: A Fan Experience...', undated. Available online at http://www.vluvshahrukh.com/exclusive/warwick/. (downloaded on 28 July 2007). SRK was at Warwick Castle to inaugurate its newest attraction, 'Dream of Battle', on 20 June 2007.
18. Stalking (etymologically connected, interestingly, to stealing!) celebrities is a well-known phenomenon in the UK and USA. Gwyneth Paltrow, Naomi Campbell, Sheryl Crow have all filed famous stalking cases in their careers. Legally speaking, many states (California, for example) in the USA treat stalking as 'invasion of privacy'. The most famous stalker is perhaps John Hinckley who, after failing to interest actress Jodie Foster despite persistent stalking, shot President Ronald Reagan in order to impress her! In the USA the problem is serious enough to warrant a full organisation, Stalking Resource Center (supported by the Office on Violence Against Women under the US Department of Justice). The Kevin Kostner-Whitney Houston film, *The Bodyguard* (1992), was about a stalker. In India we have crank callers who trouble celebrities on the phone. In recent times one Miraz Rehman (alias Naved Don) was arrested in Hyderabad for making obscene phone calls and SMSs to a variety of Bollywood actors—Priyanka Chopra, Kareena Kapoor, Nagma, Kangana Ranaut, and others. 'Bollywood Crank Caller Held', *Deccan Chronicle*, 30 July 2007, p. 1. Shah Rukh Khan's major success, *Darr* (1993) portrayed him as a stalker. On stalkers see Rojek, 2001: 64–8.

19. A PDF version of the letterhead can be found at *http://www. cscsarchive.org/MediaArchive/art.nsf/. 29 July 2007.*
20. See http://www.cscsarchive.org/MediaArchive/art.nsf/. 29 July 2007.
21. Equally clueless parents, catch up on Power Rangers at *http:// disney.go.com/powerrangers/home.html.*
22. It is interesting to note, therefore, that celebrity author JK Rowling asserts great control over any information (including academic works) produced about Harry Potter. Websites have to first clear their information with her offices. Rowling's attempt to regulate information is a radical new attempt to determine what can be said about her creation. As noted elsewhere in this book, everything in the Rowling industry seeks to emphasise and reinforce the stature and power of the author.
23. Fan culture itself may be subversive and resistant to official power. A good example of this, as Sandvoss (2005: 33) points out, is the football fans of England.
24. For a collection see *http://trekfanfiction.net/.* For studies of fan fiction see Jenkins (1992).
25. A particularly interesting example of fan fiction is slash fiction— fiction that involves male characters from an 'original' story in a romantic, homoerotic, even homosexual relationship in new plots. Mostly written by women, slash fiction is believed to have begun with fan fiction depicting Kirk and Spock of *Star Trek* in such a relationship. For studies of this exciting genre within fan fiction see Kustritz (2003), Thrupkaew (2003), Shave (2004), Jung (2005) and Woledge (2005). There is now slash fiction involving Harry Potter and Draco Malfoy.
26. http://www.epicindia.com/Original-Fiction/warriors-of-dandaka-praambha (downloaded on 27 July 2007). The magazine does not carry a date of issue/posting, though Karniak/Karnick's blog identifies the first posting of the story as 27 February 2006.
27. In a study of celebrity advocacy, Thomas Goodnight (2005) proposes that celebrity work in politics is a mix of televisualised criticism and the 'stylistic vision of film production', and even supplemented the truncated Presidential debates of 2004. Thus celebrity advocacy must be seen as a significant component of deliberative democracy.

Conclusion: The New Cool
of Celebrity Culture

It is important to see celebrity culture as a complex phenomenon that situates some people, events and *places simultaneously distant and intimate* from us. SRK is a stranger whose lifestyle, family, food preferences are familiar to us. My thesis is that the *celebrity culture is looped back into everyday life when the world of glamour and power, otherwise distant to us, acquires an unusual familiarity.* The distant world of film and sports stars is rooted in our everyday lives, a constituent of our visual fields from hoardings to TV. In terms borrowed from social theory, *celebrity culture is recursively linked to the material everyday lives of millions of people who move, live, entertain, clothe themselves in the presence, via mediated images, of celebrities.*

Celebrity culture is a very visible, significant and commercially viable component of a society's public culture today. Culture itself is taken to mean both, a way of life and the set of practices, institutions and structures of power that constantly negotiate meanings, where, through processes of inclusion and exclusion, some meanings, groups and 'texts' get valorised at the expense of others. Studies of cultural artifacts and processes, such as film, folk, art, television and, in this case, celebrity, involves a *political* reading of structures of power that influence, and often determine, meaning-production in a culture, focussing on groups that are disempowered and subalternised in cultural practices. This means looking at questions of *agency, genealogy* and, finally, *identity* and *power*. Agency signifies the capability of individuals, communities or objects to assert their will and effect changes. Genealogy is the location of a particular technology or cultural artifact within its specific history, discourses and power struggles. Identities are seen as *constructs* rather than immanent, as *negotiated* rather than self-evident.

From such a perspective, celebrities are the effect of multiple negotiations and interactions. They might be unique individuals, but their celebrity-effect is not the consequence of their uniqueness alone. The celebrity is situated at the *intersection of numerous discourses—merit, attractiveness, social power and influence and taste*, all of which are located within a structure of capitalist production and consumption. This complex intersection that produces celebrity culture is what this book has called *celebrity ecology*. The notion of celebrity ecology underscores the fact that the celebrity is not the effect of any one predominant element, whether it is material culture, organisations or social discourses, but of all of these. As in an ecological environment or bio-system there is a mutually dependent, symbiotic relationship between the elements within that system. Celebrity ecology looks at the environment of the celebrity *as a whole*, where the various elements in the environment interact with each other to produce the *celebrity effect*. Celebrity culture can only be studied through celebrity *ecology* for the simple reason that celebrities are the result of many forms of interaction between multiple discourses, technologies, flows and sites. Celebrity culture is not one but many. Hence the approach cannot be one but many.

A celebrity possesses a certain amount of agency by virtue of the very structure of her or his production and consumption. Agency is the celebrity's ability to appropriate and be appropriated by these discourses, to be marketed and consumed as a commodity that generates profits, both economic and social (by which I mean non-quantifiable forms of wealth like influence, prestige and trend-setting).

Their *ability* to negotiate with systems of representation—mass media, spectacle and institutions—generates public interest in them. This is the question of *agency* where the unique individual's ability is harnessed to a system of signification, such as structures that generate meaning through advertisements and images. Celebrities often therefore train themselves in and ready themselves for the art of self-representation through finishing schools, dance and speech training, fashion, among others. Thus their uniqueness and media glamour, what we have described here as agency, is itself the effect of multiple processes.

These processes are, more often than not, and especially in the case of film or sports stars, driven by commercial interests. Celebrity management is a thriving business enterprise today. Celebrity culture must be therefore located within this capitalist system of selling individuals as unique by generating an interest in their uniqueness. The individual's qualities are marketed, publicised and sold in order to generate profits for the film, the music album, the tournament or the brand being endorsed. It is therefore important to locate celebrity culture and the celebrity's agency within a system of what I termed *meritocratic capitalism* where the presumed or real merit, a term I use to describe numerous qualities of stars, including looks, intelligence, talent, power, is linked to massive profits. This is of course a *materialist* reading of celebrity culture, but one, I believe, that necessarily foregrounds the commercial-capitalist dimension of stars. We need to see celebrities as part of processes that enable the construction of particular skills as desirable so that profits are generated.

However, celebrities are not simply agents of profit-making. Celebrity philanthropists and activists, such as Medha Patkar, and more recently, Dr Rajendra Pachauri, are agents of social change and consciousness-raising. In this case agency is the ability of the celebrity to muster social support, alter the terms of the debate and open up the public sphere. Here celebrity culture is linked to questions of the public sphere, democratisation and power, where the celebrity's agency is instrumental in altering each of these *social* aspects.

Instead of treating the celebrity as simply an exceptional individual, we need to locate her or him within those *structures*, within a culture that generate what can be called the *discourse of quality and merit*. How are particular talents treated as valuable? Why is, for instance, a talented cricketer paid more, and earns more than a talented hockey player (hockey, incidentally, being our national game)? How does cricket become the key commercialised sport in India and its practitioners, celebrities? This involves looking at questions of institutions (the Board of Cricket Control for India, the International Cricket Council, the global tournaments, the structure of internal tournaments), of state funding, endorsements and recognition and the cult of a Tendulkar. A genealogical perspective looks at the horizontal and vertical structures, like sports, films, that create discourses of talent or quality. Who funds the promos of a film? What agencies and institutions are involved in promoting a tournament? What is the *history* of a particular sport or film or artifact? Who contributed to its making and remaking? Who made a profit out of the particular valorised skill? What communities, classes or castes take to particular sports?

A good example of such a genealogical reading that looks at celebrity sports stars is available in Ramachandra Guha's *A Corner of a Foreign Field: The Indian History of a British Sport* (2002). Guha, himself a celebrity historian today, with the patient teasing out of discourses we associate with social history, looks at the celebrated cricketer C.K. Nayudu, often thought of as India's first great cricketer. Guha suggests that Nayudu attained this celebrity status because the social structures of India at that time did not and could not think beyond caste. Palwankar Baloo, a *Dalit*, was India's first great cricketer, argues Guha, but the social structures ensured that his name would never figure in the honour list. Playing for his team, the Poona Hindus, Palwankar Baloo distinguished himself on the field, but was served his meals at a separate table. What is interesting is to see how social conditions affect a player's celebrity status where the skill becomes less significant than the player's caste. The Dalit player is disempowered, the meanings he generates on the field become marginal when the mainstream history of Indian cricket is written and evoked. Baloo does not figure in celebrity players' lists nor does he trigger a memory even for the connoisseur. Baloo moves away from the visual, historical or visibility field because he is a Dalit. Clearly, celebrity visibility is linked to caste, regional and religious identity. This is genealogical criticism where institutions, social codes and conditions and power struggles are foregrounded when reading a particular artifact or phenomenon.

The question of agency or capacity and visibility is intimately linked, also, to questions of identity and power. Celebrities command social-symbolic and economic power, as underscored throughout this book. Their identity *as* celebrities generate income, profits, influence and has social impact. However, this identity, whether of Tendulkar's or JLo's, is not an immanent feature, but the effect of a series of negotiations. Identity is a construct, and multiple discourses, structures and practices contribute to the making of a celebrity identity. To begin with, as noted above, there are the marketing and celebrity management industries. A careful positioning of the individual and her or his skills ensures that particular aspects of the individual are highlighted and others downplayed. Comparative assessments with other individuals are used to show why X or Y is superior or different. Then the individual is promoted as the icon of those qualities that are deemed to be desirable. Identity here is the result of a complex series of manoeuvres and negotiations where a set of qualities—looks, commitment, skill—are promoted as desirable and are then linked to the individual. It is not a simple cause-effect scheme of desirable talent leading to the discovery of a celebrity who possesses that talent or vice versa.

Celebrity identity can be best described as an effect generated by the system of *flows* of capital, image and representations, discourses of talents and skills. It involves questions of power where capital plays an important role. How much finance is needed to produce a celebrity brand? What profits does SRK generate for AIRTEL? How does society treat or look up to him or Dhoni and, therefore, what kind of symbolic or cultural capital do they possess?

Celebrity ecology moves between the figure of the celebrity through the marketing, circulation and consumption mechanisms that make this figure *a part of our lives* (pin-ups of SRK and Tendulkar, and Ram Guha on the coffee table, and Dhoni hairstyles in hairdressing salons) even as they stay distant from us.

The marketing agencies, the film industry, the sports industry, including sports goods manufacturers who shell out vast amounts of endorsements fees to Michael Jordan and Tendulkar, the numerous awards and their widely televised ceremonies, which themselves showcase new celebrities and profits, constitute the *main* structures that frame celebrity culture.

Once the product is made by the marketing agencies then the film, TV, Internet and other forms of media take over. These circulate particular kinds of images of the celebrity. The *content* of these representations, which could range from product endorsements to interviews and photo-shoots of film stars' homes, might be generated by the media structures, but their work is very different. They serve up particular images of icons—the reliable Dravid, the flamboyant Beckham and the socially committed Patkar. The content of circulating representations is highly controlled and monitored for this purpose. This is the reason why celebrities do not want to be caught doing things that do not fit in with their image.

The content is absorbed by an audience, whose nature, demographics and desires cannot always be predicted. Here the *impact* of the first two components of celebrity ecology, structures and content, is crucial. What kind of image does Dhoni project (youth icon)? What does the famous LIC logo stand for (security, family)? Impact here is the kind of value system being promoted and absorbed by the audience.

None of these are independent elements, but work in tandem to produce the celebrity effect. There is, with the information technology revolution, increasing web presence and archiving of celebrity news, thereby extending the realm and influence of the celebrity. This constitutes yet another technology of celebrification. The important thing with studies of celebrity culture is to see how celebrities affect *our* perception of the world, perceptions that include admiration, belief in virtue rewarded, skill, competition, financial success, because of the celebrity's own success and *representation* of this success. The celebrity is at the intersection of economic and social activities, where celebrity culture is itself a *networked environment* within which each of the items described above serves as a node through which celebrity flows. It is in the *interaction* of these multiple nodes and flows that the celebrity is produced. Marketing agencies, profits, value systems (individualism, social commitment and consumerism), fans and audiences, material objects (pin-up posters, music albums, film and fashion), technology are all interconnected in their contribution to the making of the celebrity. These are the elements that put SRK on our TV screen, intrude into our sound world as songs or voice, and entertain you when you take your child for a haircut.

Celebrity ecology helps us locate the representation, the hero, the fan within an environment where marketing, rhetoric, media technologies intersect and construct the celebrity. It asks that we pay attention to the material, non-material, political and discursive contexts of celebrity culture. Celebrity ecology links the body or face of the celebrity with the cultural industry, the mass media, the technologies of cosmetics, transmission or archiving, the political economy of the celebrity's chosen field such as sport, television, cinema, politics.

Celebrity culture is everywhere. We live in the midst of it. Everyone is tired of seeing the celebrity around (all newspaper pages now seem to have morphed into P3), but no one seems to quite know how to get rid of it. And yet everyone wants a slice of it. The mechanisms of contemporary cultural production, what I have described as celebrity ecology, ensure that celebrity culture is the new cool of our lives.

So now: who wants to be a celebrity?

Bibliography

Abercrombie, N. and B. Longhurst. 1998. *Audiences: A Sociological Theory of Performance and Imagination*. London: Sage.

Ahmed, Z. 2007. 'Dream Home of India's Richest Man', BBC News, 1 June. Available online at http://news.bbc.co.uk/2/hi/south_asia/6712605.stm (downloaded on 04.11.2007).

Alexander, S.M. 2003. 'Stylish Hard Bodies: Branded Masculinity in "Men's Health" Magazine', *Sociological Perspectives*, 46 (4): 535–54.

Almeida, A. 2007. 'Indian Idol Ka Magic Chalega Kya?', Interview, *GR8! TV Mag*, June 2007.

Alter, J.S. 2004. 'Body, Text, Nation: Writing the Physically Fit Body in Post-Colonial India', in J.H. Mills and S. Sen (eds), *Confronting the Body: The Politics of Physicality in Colonial and Post-Colonial India*, pp. 16–38. London: Anthem.

Anusha, I.R. 2007. 'Celebrity-Struck', *The Hindu*, Metroplus, 26 July. Available online at http://www.hinduonnet.com/thehindu/mp/2007/07/26/stories/2007072650030100.htm (downloaded on 27.01.2008).

Astroff, R.J. and A.K. Nyberg. 1992. 'Discursive Hierarchies and the Construction of Crisis in the News: A Case Study', *Discourse and Society*, 3 (1): 5–24.

Auslander, P. 1999. *Liveness: Performance in a Mediatized Culture*. London and New York: Routledge.

Barbour, R. 2003. *Before Orientalism: London's Theatre of the East, 1570–1626*. Cambridge: Cambridge University Press.

BBC Sport Football. 2007. 'Beckham Agrees to LA Galaxy Move', 12 January. Available online at http://news.bbc.co.uk/sport2/hi/football/6248835.stm (downloaded on 15.09.2007).

Benjamin, W. 2002 (1921). 'Critique of Violence', Edmund Jephcott (tr.), in Marcus Bullock and Michael W. Jennings (eds), *Walter Benjamin: Selected Writings, Vol. I, 1913–1926*, pp. 236–52. Cambridge, MA: Belknap Press of Harvard University Press.

Bhatt, S. 2006. 'Lalu Comes to IIM-A with New Image', 18 September. Available online at http://www.rediff.com (downloaded on 24.05.2007).

Bhattacharya, C.S. 2005. 'Death of a Star, Unseen and Unsung', *The Telegraph*, 23 January. Available online at http://www.telegraphindia.com/1050123/asp/frontpage/story_4287832.asp (downloaded on 07.07.2007).

Bhattacharya, I. 2007. 'Watch TV Serials on Your Cellphones', 9, 25 May, p. 23.

Bhatnagar, M. 2007. 'Matters of Marital Discord', *Society*, June, pp. 111–5.

Bird, S.E. 2003. *The Audience in Everyday Life: Living in a Media World*. London and New York: Routledge.

Biressi, A. 2004. '"Above the Below": Body Trauma as Spectacle in Social/Media Space', *Journal for Cultural Research*, 8 (3): 335–52.

Biressi, A. and H. Nunn. 2003. 'The Especially Remarkable: Celebrity and Social Mobility in Reality TV', *Mediactive*, 2: 44–58.

Blake, D.H. 2001. 'Public Dreams: Berryman, Celebrity, and the Culture of Confession', *American Literary History*, 13 (4): 716–36.

Boorstin, D.J. 1961. *The Image: A Guide to Pseudo-Events in America*. New York: Harper Colophon.

Bordo, S. 1990. *Unbearable Weight: Feminism, Western Culture and the Body*. Berkeley, CA: University of California Press.

Botta, R.A. 1999. 'Television Images and Adolescent Girls' Body Image Disturbance', *Journal of Communication*, 49 (2): 22–41.

Boyle, K. 2005. *Media and Violence*. London: Sage Publications.

Braudy, L. 1986. *The Frenzy of Renown: Fame and Its History*. New York: Oxford University Press.

Brijnath, R. undated. 'Little Big Man.' Available online at http://www.india-today.com/itoday/millennium/100people/sachin.html (downloaded on 15.09.2007).

Brooker, W. 2000. *Batman Unmasked: The Making of a Cultural Icon*. New York and London: Continuum.

Cashmore, E. 2006. *Celebrity/Culture*. London and New York Routledge.

Choi, S.M. and N.J. Rifon. 2007. 'Who is the Celebrity in Advertising? Understanding Dimensions of Celebrity Images', *Journal of Popular Culture*, 40 (2): 304–24.

Chopra, A. 2007. *King of Bollywood: Shah Rukh Khan and the Seductive World of Indian Cinema*. New York: Warner.

Chougule. 2007. 'Singer No. 1', *Deccan Chronicle*, TV Entertainment Guide, 15 September, p. 1.

Chunduri, M. 2006. 'Digital Distractions', *The Times of India*, 27 November. Available online at http://timesofindia.indiatimes.com/articleshow/589301.cms (downloaded on 25.07.2007).

Clerc, S. 2002. 'Estrogen Brigades and "Big Tits" Threads: Media Fandom On-line and Off', in D. Bell and B.M. Kennedy (eds), *The Cybercultures Reader*, pp. 216–29. London: Routledge.

Cloete, E. 2003. 'Specificities: An "Eye" for an "I": Discipline and Gossip', *Social Identities*, 9 (3): 401–22.

Conlan, T. 2007. 'Channel 4 Praised for Big Brother Action', *The Guardian*, 7 June. Available online at http://media.guardian.co.uk/bigbrother/story/0,2097741,00.html (downloaded on 31.07.2007).

Couldry, N. 2003. *Media Rituals: A Critical Approach*. London and New York: Routledge.

Critcher, C. 2003. *Moral Panics and the Media*. Buckingham, UK: Open University Press.

D'Ancona, M. 2007. '10 Years Later: Diana and the Queen', *The Spectator*, reprinted in *Deccan Chronicle*, 2 September, p. 7.

David, R. 2006. 'India's Celebrity Divorces', *Forbes*, 19 December. Available online at http://www.forbes.com/digitalentertainment/2006/12/19/india-bollywood-divorce-tech-media-cx_rd_1219indiadivorce.html (downloaded on 27.01.2008).

Davies, J. 2001. *Diana, A Cultural History: Gender, Race, Nation and the People's Princess*. London: Palgrave.

Day, J. 2002. 'Channel 4: Thinks Big for Celebrity Reality Show', *The Guardian*, 4 November. Available online at http://media.guardian.co.uk/bigbrother/story/0,829984,00.html (downloaded on 31.07.2007).

Dayan, D. and E. Katz. 1992. *Media Events: The Live Broadcasting of History*. Cambridge, MA: Harvard University Press.

Deccan Chronicle. 2007. 'Why Bachchans didn't Call Them', *Deccan Chronicle*, Hyderabad Chronicle, 20 April, pp. 21 and 23.

Dickinson, K. 2003. 'Pop Stars Who can't Act', *Mediactive*, 2: 74–85.

Diekema, D.A. 1991. 'Televangelism and the Mediated Charismatic Relationship', *Social Science Journal*, 28 (2): 143–62.

Dutton, K.R. 1995. *The Perfectible Body: The Western Ideal of Physical Development*. London: Cassell.

Dwyer, A. 2004. 'Disorder or Delight: Towards a New Account of the Fashion Model Body', *Fashion Theory*, 8 (4): 405–24.

Dyer, R. 1986. *Heavenly Bodies: Film Stars and Society*. London: British Film Institute and St. Martin's Press.

———. 2002. *Stars*. London: British Film Institute.

Eatwell, R. 2006. 'The Concept and Theory of Charismatic Leadership', *Totalitarian Movements and Political Religions*, 7 (2): 141–56.

Edensor, T. 1998. *Tourists at the Taj*. London: Sage Publications.

Eisenstein, E. 1979. *The Printing Press as an Agent of Change: Communications and Cultural Transformation in Early-Modern Europe*, 2 vols. Cambridge: Cambridge University Press.

Elliott, A. 1998. 'Celebrity and Political Psychology: Remembering John Lennon', *Political Psychology*, 19 (4): 833–52.

Egner, J. 2007. 'The New Definition of "Sexy".' Available online at http://
lifestyle.msn.com/relationships/articlepage.aspx?cp-documentid=
8415525 (downloaded on 03.12.2008).

Entwhistle, J. 2000. *The Fashioned Body: Fashion, Dress and Modern
Social Theory*. Cambridge: Polity.

Evans, D. 1996. *An Introductory Dictionary of Lacanian Psychoanalysis*. Available online at http://web.nwe.ufl.edu/elf/conf98/
extimacy.html (downloaded on 12.06.2008)

Fairchild, C. 2007. 'Building the Authentic Celebrity: The "Idol" Phenomenon in the Attention Economy', *Popular Music and Society*, 30 (3):
355–75.

Feasey, R. 2006. 'Get a Famous Body: Star Styles and Celebrity Gossip
in *heat* Magazine', in S. Holmes and S. Redmond (eds), *Framing
Celebrity: New Directions in Celebrity Culture*, pp. 177–94. London
and New York: Routledge.

Featherstone, M. 1991. *Consumer Culture and Postmodernism*. London:
Sage.

Ferris, K.O. 2004. 'Seeing and Being Seen: The Moral Order of Celebrity
Sightings', *Journal of Contemporary Ethnography*, 33 (3): 236–64.

Fiske, J. 1987. *Television Culture*. London: Routledge.

———. 1992. 'The Cultural Economy of Fandom', in L.A. Lewis (ed.),
The Adoring Audience, pp. 37–42. London: Routledge.

Fox, R. 2006. 'Jesus as Celebrity', *The Journal of American and Canadian
Studies*, 24: 3–16.

Franco, J. 2006. 'Langsters Online: K.D. Lang and the Creation of Internet Fan Communities', in S. Holmes and S. Redmond (eds), *Framing
Celebrity: New Directions in Celebrity Culture*, pp. 269–83. London
and New York: Routledge.

Frow, J. 1998. 'Is Elvis a God? Cult, Culture, Questions of Method', *International Journal of Cultural Studies*, 1 (2): 197–210.

———. 2002. 'Signature and Brand', in J. Collins (ed.), *High-Pop:
Making Culture into Popular Entertainment*, pp. 56–74. Malden,
MA: Blackwell.

Gamson, J. 2001. 'The Assembly Line of Greatness: Celebrity in
Twentieth-Century America', in C.L. Harrington and D.D. Bielby
(eds), *Popular Culture: Production and Consumption*, pp. 259–82.
Oxford: Blackwell.

Geraghty, C. and C. Lusted (eds). 1998. *The Television Studies Book*.
London: Arnold.

Gilbert, J. 2004. 'Small Faces: The Tyranny of Celebrity in Post-Oedipal
Culture', *Mediactive*, 2: 86–109.

Glaister, D. 2007. 'Now, Children Drink Bleach on Reality TV', *The
Guardian*, reprinted in *The Hindu*, 18 September, p. 11.

Goffman, E. 1969. *The Presentation of Self in Everyday Life*. London: Allen Lane.

Goldman, L., M. Burke, and K. Blakeley. 2007. 'The Celebrity 100', *Forbes* 179.1, 2 July, p. 82.

Goodnight, T.G. 2005. '*The Passion of the Christ* Meets *Fahrenheit 9/11*: A Study in Celebrity Advocacy', *American Behavioral Scientist*, 49 (3): 410–35.

Gotham, K.F. 2005. 'Theorizing Urban Spectacles: Festivals, Tourisms and the Transformation of Urban Space', *City*, 9 (2): 225–46.

Gray, C.H. 1997. *Postmodern War: The New Politics of Conflict*. London: Routledge.

GR8! TV Mag. 2007. 'Indian Idol ka Magic Chalega Kya?', *GR 8! TV Mag*, June, p. 72.

Grindstaff, L. 1997. 'Producing Trash, Class and the Money Shot', in J. Lull and S. Hinerman (eds), *Media Scandals*. Cambridge: Polity Press.

Grixti, J. 1995. 'Consuming Cannibals: Psychopathic Killers as Archetypes and Cultural Icons', *Journal of American Culture*, 18 (1): 87–96.

Guha, R. 2002. *A Corner of a Foreign Field: The Indian History of a British Sport*. Delhi: Picador.

Haralovich, M.B. and M.W. Trosset. 2004. '"Expect the Unexpected": Narrative Pleasure and Uncertainty Due to Chance in *Survivor*', in L. Ouellette and S. Murray (eds), *Reality TV: Remaking Television Culture*, pp. 75–96. New York: New York University Press.

Harper, S. 2006. 'Madly Famous: Narratives of Mental Illness in Celebrity Culture', in S. Holmes and S. Redmond (eds), *Framing Celebrity: New Directions in Celebrity Culture*, pp. 310–27. London: Routledge.

Helmers, M. 2001. 'Media, Discourse, and the Public Sphere: Electronic Memorials to Diana, Princess of Wales', *College English*, 63 (4): 437–56.

Hermes, J. 1999. 'Media Figures in Identity Construction', in P. Alasuutari (ed.), *Rethinking the Media Audience: The New Agenda*, pp. 69–85. London: Sage.

Hetsroni, A. 2005. 'Globalization and Knowledge Hierarchy through the Eyes of a Quiz Show: A Cross-Cultural Analysis of Who Wants to be a Millionaire in North America, West Europe, East Europe and Saudi Arabia', *Innovation*, 18 (4): 385–405.

Hills, M. 2003. '"Subcultural Celebrity" and Cult TV Fan Cultures', *Mediactive*, 2, pp. 59–73.

———. 2006. 'Not Just Another Powerless Elite?: When Media Fans Become Subcultural Celebrities', in S. Holmes and S. Redmond (eds), *Framing Celebrity: New Directions in Celebrity Culture*, pp. 101–18. London and New York: Routledge.

Holmes, S. and S. Redmond (eds). 2006. *Framing Celebrity: New Directions in Celebrity Culture*. London and New York: Routledge.

Izod, J. 2001. *Myth, Mind and the Screen: Understanding the Heroes of Our Time*. Cambridge: Cambridge University Press.

Jacob, S. 2007. 'Virginia Shooting Revives Debate on Gun Control', 23 April. Available online at http://www.ndtv.com/convergence/ndtv/story.aspx?id=NEWEN20070009540 (downloaded on 13.07.2007).

Jenkins, H. 1992. *Textual Poachers: Television Fans and Participatory Culture*. New York and London: Routledge.

Jensen, J. 2001. 'Fandom as Pathology: The Consequences of Characterization', in C.L. Harrington and D.D. Bielby (eds), *Popular Culture: Production and Consumption*, pp. 301–14. Oxford: Blackwell.

Jewkes, Y. 2004. *Media and Crime*. London: Sage.

Jha, S.K. 2005. 'Gosh, so many films with her!', 27 January. Available online at http://in.rediff.com/movies/2005/jan/27pb1.htm (downloaded on 07.07.2007).

Jung, S. 2004. 'Queering Popular Culture: Female Spectators and the Appeal of Writing Slash Fan Fiction', Gender Forum 8. Available online at http://www.genderforum.uni-koeln.de/queer/jung.html (downloaded on 06.02.2008).

Kamins, M.A., M.J. Brand, S.A. Hoeke, and J.C. Moe. 1989. 'Two-sided Versus One-sided Celebrity Endorsements: The Impact on Advertising Effectiveness and Credibility', *Journal of Advertising*, 18 (2): 4–10.

Kear, A. and D.L. Steinberg (eds). 1999. *Mourning Diana: Nation, Culture and the Performance of Grief*. New York: Routledge.

Keller, E.F. 2002. *The Century of the Gene*. Cambridge, MA: Harvard University Press.

Kellner, D. 2003. *Media Spectacle*. London and New York: Routledge.

Kershaw, B. 1996. 'The Politics of Postmodern Performance', in P. Campell (ed.), *Analysing Performance: A Critical Reader*. Manchester, UK: Manchester University Press.

Khan, S.R. 2003. 'Interview with Anupama Chopra, *India Today*'. Available online at www.anupamachopra.com/a-it/srk2 (downloaded on 06.04.2008).

Kooistra, P. 1989. *Criminals as Heroes: Structure, Power, and Identity*. Bowling Green, OH: Bowling Green University Popular Press.

Kurian, A. 2008. 'On Celebrity Culture'. Personal Communication.

Kustritz, A. 2003. 'Slashing the Romance Narrative', *Journal of American Culture*, 26: 371–84.

Lambiase, J. 2003. 'Codes of Online Sexuality: Celebrity, Gender and Marketing on the Web', *Sexuality and Culture*, 7 (3): 57–78.

Lavakare, A. 2007. 'Today's India has a New Culture', 25 April. Available online at http://www.rediff.com/news/2007/apr/25arvind.htm (downloaded on 15.09.2007).

Lepsius, M.R. 2006. 'The Model of Charismatic Leadership and the Applicability to the Rule of Adolf Hitler', *Totalitarian Movements and Political Religions*, 7 (2): 175–90.

Levine, M. 2006. 'Paris Hilton says DUI arrest "was nothing"', Associated Press, 7 September 2006. Available online at http://www.msnbc.msn.com/id/14712866 (downloaded on 15.09.2007).

Leyton, E. 1986. *Hunting Humans: The Rise of the Modern Multiple Murderer*. Toronto: McClelland and Stewart.

Lines, G. 2001. 'Villains, Fools or Heroes? Sports Stars as Role Models for Young People', *Leisure Studies*, 20: 285–303.

Littler, J. 2003. 'Making Fame Ordinary: Intimacy, Reflexivity and "Keeping it Real"', *Mediactive*, 2: 8–25.

MacDougall, J.P. 2003. 'Transnational Commodities as Local Cultural Icons: Barbie Dolls in Mexico', *Journal of Popular Culture*, 37 (2): 257–75.

Mailer, Norman. 1981. '"Discovering Jack H. Abbott" and Jack Henry Abbott, "Two Notes by Jack H. Abbott"', *New York Review of Books*, 28 (10), 11 July.

Majumdar, B. 2004. *Twenty-two Yards to Freedom: A Social History of Indian Cricket*. Delhi: Penguin.

Marks, M.P. and Z.M. Fischer. 2002. 'The King's New Bodies: Simulating Consent in the Age of Celebrity', *New Political Science*, 24 (3): 371–94.

Marshall, P.D. 1997. *Celebrity and Power: Fame in Contemporary Culture*. Minneapolis, MN: University of Minnesota Press.

———. 2002. 'The Cinematic Apparatus and the Construction of the Film Celebrity', in G. Turner (ed.), *The Film Cultures Reader*, pp. 228–39. London and New York: Routledge.

Masciarotte, J.G. 2004. 'C'mon, Girl: Oprah Winfrey and the Discourse of Feminine Talk', in L. Fischer and M. Landy (eds), *Stars: The Film Reader*, pp. 251–65. New York and London: Routledge.

McBeth, J. 2004. 'I couldn't forget Sobhraj', *Nepali Times*, No. 217, 8—14 October. Available online at http://www.nepalitimes.com/issue/217/Nation/1871 (downloaded on 04.04.2008).

Meyer, D.S. and J. Gamson. 1995. 'The Challenge of Cultural Elites: Celebrities and Cultural Movements', *Sociological Inquiry*, 65 (2): 181–206.

Ministry of Women and Child Development. 2007. *Report of the Committee Investigating into Allegations of Large Scale Sexual Abuse, Rape and Murder of Children in Nithari Village of Noida*, 17 January. Government of India. Available online at http://wcd.nic.in/nitharireport.pdf (downloaded on 16.09.2007).

Mirzoeff, N. 2006. 'Invisible Empire: Visual Culture, Embodied Spectacle and Abu Ghraib', *Radical History Review*, 95: 21–44.

Mishra, A. 2005. '"Cool" Babi Broke Deewar of Stereotypes', *The Times of India*, 22 January. Available online at http://timesofindia.indiatimes.com/articleshow/998600.cms (downloaded on 07.07.2007).

Moeller, S.D. 1999. *Compassion Fatigue: How the Media Sell Disease, Famine, War and Death*. New York and London: Routledge.

Mole, T. 2004. 'Hypertrophic Celebrity', *M/C* 7 (5). Available online at http://journal.media-culture.org.au/0411/08-mole.php (downloaded on 11.07.2007).

Moran, J. 2000. *Star Authors: Literary Celebrity in America*. London: Pluto.

Murray, S. and L. Ouellette (eds). 2004. *Reality TV: Remaking Television Culture*. New York: New York University Press.

Nalapat, A. and A. Parker. 2005. 'Sport, Celebrity and Popular Culture: Sachin Tendulkar, Cricket and Indian Nationalisms', *International Review for the Sociology of Sport*, 40 (4): 433–46.

Nayar, P.K. 2006. *Reading Culture: Theory, Praxis, Politics*. New Delhi: Sage Publications.

———. 2008. 'The Male Order Catalogue: Constructions of Masculinity in Men's Magazines'. Unpublished Paper. Presented at National Conference on 'Representations of Gender in Popular Literature and Film'. Sophia College for Women, Mumbai, 18–19 January 2008.

Neimark, J. 1995. 'The Culture of Celebrity', *Psychology Today*, 28 (3): 54–6, 86–7 and 90.

Nelson, C., P.A. Treichler, and L. Grossberg. 1992. 'Cultural Studies: An Introduction', in L. Grossberg, C. Nelson, and P.A. Treichler (eds), *Cultural Studies*, pp. 1–16. London and New York: Routledge.

O'Leary, S.D. 1996. 'Cyberspace as Sacred Space: Communicating Religion on Computer Networks', *Journal of the American Academy of Religion*, 64 (4): 781–808.

Ouellette, L. and S. Murray. 2004. 'Introduction', in L. Ouellette and S. Murray (eds), *Reality TV: Remaking Television Culture*, pp. 1–15. New York: New York University Press.

Pandey, D. 2007. 'Crossing Healthy Limits', *Daily News and Analysis*, After Hours Sunday, 11 August. p. 7.

Pisharoty, S.B. 2005. 'Fame in the Time of Reality TV', *The Hindu*, 25 November. Available online at http://www.hindu.com/the-hindu/fr/2005/11/25/stories/2005112501670100.htm (downloaded on 12.09.2007).

Pullen, K. 2000. 'I-Love-Xena.com': Creating Online Fan Communities', in D. Gauntlett (ed.), *Web Studies: Rewiring Media Studies for the Digital Age*, pp. 52–61. London: Arnold.

Quail, C.M., K.A. Razzano, and L.H. Skalli. 2005. *Vulture Culture: The Politics and Pedagogy of Daytime Television Talk Shows*. New York: Peter Lang.

Rak, J. 2005. 'The Digital Queer: Weblogs and Internet Identity', *Biography*, 26 (1): 166–82.

Raval, S. 2001. 'Making of *Lagaan*', *India Today*, 25 June. Available online at http://www.india-today.com/itoday/20010625/cover3.shtml (downloaded on 17.09.2007).

Reyes, O. 2003. 'Cheriegate! Celebrity, Scandal and Political Leadership', *Mediactive*, 2: 26–43.

Rojek, C. 2001. *Celebrity*. London: Reaktion.

Runkle, S. 2004. 'Making "Miss India": Constructing Gender, Power and the Nation', *South Asian Popular Culture*, 2 (2): 145–59.

Rushdie, S. 2002. 'Notes on Writing and the Nation', in *Step Across this Line: Collected Nonfiction, 1992–2002*, pp. 58–62. New York: Random House.

Sandvoss, C. 2005. *Fans: The Mirror of Consumption*. Cambridge: Polity Press.

Saxena, S. 2007. 'Porn Racket Hits Delhi School', *Hindustan Times*, 31 August. Available online at http://www.hindustantimes.com/PhotoGallery/Photos_StoryPage.aspx?Category=PornracketinDelhi (downloaded on 15.09.2007). Also available online at http://content.msn.co.in/News/National/NationalIANS_100907_1619.htm (downloaded on 15.09.2007).

Sayre, S. and C. King. 2003. *Entertainment and Society: Audiences, Trends, and Impacts*. Thousand Oaks, CA: Sage.

Schmid, D. 2006. 'Idols of Destruction: Celebrity and the Serial Killer', in S. Holmes and S. Redmond (eds), *Framing Celebrity: New Directions in Celebrity Culture*, pp. 295–310. London and New York: Routledge.

Sharma, N. 2007. 'Reality Show Winner is on the Fast Track', *Deccan Chronicle*, TV Entertainment Guide, 15 September, p. 3.

Shave, R. 2004. 'Slash Fandom on the Internet, Or Is the carnival Over?', *Refractory* 6. Available online at http://www.refractory.unimelb.edu.au/journalissues/vol6/RShave.html (downloaded on 06.02.2008).

Skoda, U. 2004. 'The Politics-Kinship Nexus in India: Sonia Gandhi *versus* Sushma Swaraj in the 1999 General Elections', *Contemporary South Asia*, 13 (3): 273–85.

Smith, J. 1998. *The Sounds of Commerce: Marketing Popular Film Music*. New York: Columbia University Press.

Sorapure, M. 2005. 'Screening Moments, Scrolling Lives: Diary Writing on the Web', *Biography*, 26 (1): 1–23.

Sridharan, J.R. 2007. 'The Girl is Now a Woman', *The Hindu*, Metroplus, 31 July, p. 1.

Stack, S. 1987. 'Celebrity and Suicide: A Taxonomy and Analysis, 1948–1983', *American Sociological Review*, 52 (3): 401–12.

Steinberg, B.S. 2005. 'Indira Gandhi: The Relationship between Personality Profile and Leadership Style', *Political Psychology*, 26 (5): 755–89.

Stickney, D. and N. Proskocil. 2007. '"Idol" Audition Crowd Thins Out in the Afternoon', *Omaha World Herald*, 9 August. Available online on http://www.omaha.com/index.php?u_page=2620&u_sid=10103018 (downloaded on 12.06.2008).

Street, J. 2004. 'Celebrity Politicians: Popular Culture and Political Representation', *British Journal of Politics and International Relations*, 6: 435–52.

Thomas, A. 2006. 'Fan Fiction Online: Engagement, Critical Response and Affective Play through Writing', *Australian Journal of Language and Literacy*, 29 (3): 226–39.

Thomas, C. 2007. 'Power of the Diana Cult', *International Herald Tribune*, reprinted in *Deccan Chronicle*, 4 September, p. 7.

Toshniwal, C. 2007. 'Celebs Turn Vegan for Love', *Deccan Chronicle*, Hyderabad Chronicle, 4 August, p. 21.

Thrupkaew, N. 2003. 'Fan/tastic Voyage: A Journey into the Wide, Wild World of Slash Fiction', in *Bitch: Feminist Response to Pop Culture* p. 20. Available inline at http://www.bitchmagazine.com/archives/04_03slash/slash.shtml (downloaded on 06.02.2008).

Turner, G. 1999. 'Tabloidisation, Journalism and the Possibility of Critique', *International Journal of Cultural Studies*, 2 (1): 59–76.

———. 2004. *Understanding Celebrity*. London: Sage.

Urry, J. 1990. *The Tourist Gaze*. London: Sage.

Wax, E. 2007. 'In India's New Consumerism, One Star Has the Most Currency', *Washington Post*, 12 August. Available online at http://www.washingtonpost.com/wp-dyn/content/article/2007/08/10/AR2007081000526.html?referrer=emailarticle (downloaded on 27.01.2008).

Whannel, G. 2002. *Media Sport Stars: Masculinities and Moralities*. London and New York: Routledge.

Wheaton, B. 2007. 'After Sport Culture: Rethinking Sport and Post-Subcultural Theory', *Journal of Sport and Social Issues*, 31(3): 283–307.

Wilkes, R. 2002. *Scandal: A Scurrilous History of Gossip*. London: Atlantic.

Williams, J. 2006. '"Protect Me from What I Want": Football Fandom, Celebrity Cultures and "New" Football in England', *Soccer and Society*, 7 (1): 96–114.

Woledge, E. 2005. 'Decoding Desire: From Kirk and Spock to K/S', *Social Semiotics*, 15: 235–50.

Zeitlin, S.J. 1979. 'Pop Lore: The Aesthetic Principles in Celebrity Gossip', *Journal of American Culture*, 2 (2): 186–92.

Zhou, David. (2006). 'Student's Novel Faces Plagiarism Controversy?', *The Harvard Crimson*, 23 April. Available online at www.thecrimson. com/archives (downloaded on 06.02.2008).

Index

About the Author

Pramod K. Nayar teaches at the Department of English, University of Hyderabad, India. His work in postcolonial studies includes *English Writing and India, 1600–1920: Colonizing Aesthetics* (2008), *Postcolonial Literature: An Introduction* (2008), *The Great Uprising: India, 1857* (2007), *The Trial of Bahadur Shah Zafar* (2007) and *The Penguin 1857 Reader* (2007).

His interests in cultural studies include superheroes, consumer culture, 'cool', posthumanism and new media cultures, and his work here includes *An Introduction to Cultural Studies* (2008), *Reading Culture: Theory, Praxis, Politics* (2006), *Virtual Worlds: Culture and Politics in the Age of Cybertechnology* (2004), and a book on literary and cultural theory (*Literary Theory Today*, 2002), besides numerous essays on cyberculture and, more recently, on human rights narratives. Among forthcoming books are a study of new media and cyberculture, postcolonialism, a history of the Raj and an edited collection on English life in India.

He can be reached electronically at pramodknayar@gmail.com.